PAST THE END OF THE ROAD

Michel Drouin

PAST
THE
END
OF THE
ROAD

A North Island Boyhood

**HARBOUR
PUBLISHING**

Harbour Publishing Co. Ltd.
P.O. Box 219, Madeira Park, BC, V0N 2H0
www.harbourpublishing.com

Edited by Brian Lynch
Cover photo courtesy Michel Drouin
Cover and text design by Dwayne Dobson
Map by Roger Handling / Terra Firma Digital Arts
Printed and bound in Canada
Printed on 100% recycled paper

Harbour Publishing acknowledges the support of the Canada Council for the
Arts, the Government of Canada, and the Province of British Columbia through
the BC Arts Council.

Library and Archives Canada Cataloguing in Publication

Title: Past the end of the road : a North Island boyhood / Michel Drouin.
Names: Drouin, Michel (Joseph Jules Michel), author.
Identifiers: Canadiana (print) 2024029033X | Canadiana (ebook) 20240293215 |
ISBN 9781990776670
 (softcover) | ISBN 9781990776687 (EPUB)
Subjects: LCSH: Drouin, Michel (Joseph Jules Michel)—Childhood and youth. |
LCSH: Port Hardy (B.C.)—
 Biography. | LCGFT: Autobiographies.
Classification: LCC FC3845.P66 D76 2024 | DDC 971.1/2—dc23

This book is dedicated to the memory of my parents Jules and Rita, and for my grandchildren Clara and Niklas.

"Lots More Men in Town"

I remember the first day I went down to the job,
The greenest kid you've ever seen around
The guys said, "Boy, you'd better watch your ass
There's lots more men in town"

Kept my eyes open wide and I learned my trade
I got pretty good at what I did
I seen men come and I seen men go
'Cause there's lots more men in town

There's lots more men in town, by God
They're pounding the streets looking for a job
Don't stand in the bight or get your ass in a sling
Because there's lots more men in town

The boss said, "Son, y'know I like your style
Keep it up and you can run the show"
He fired better men than I knew I was
Because there's lots more men in town

And then one day I got the strawline in the neck
The boss came over, I thought I'm saved
And as I lay bleeding all my life's blood on the ground
He said, "There's lots more men in town"

Contents

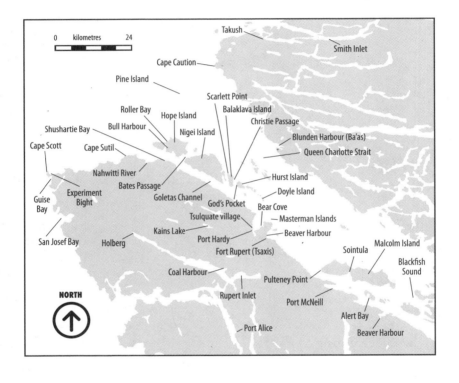

Takush

Smith Inlet

Cape Caution

Pine Island

Scarlett Point

Roller Bay
Hope Island
Balaklava Island

Shushartie Bay
Bull Harbour
Christie Passage

Cape Scott
Nigei Island
Blunden Harbour (Ba'as)

Cape Sutil
Queen Charlotte Strait

Nahwitti River

Guise
Bay
Experiment
Bight
Bates Passage
Goletas Channel
Hurst Island

Doyle Island

God's Pocket
Bear Cove

Tsulquate village
Masterman Islands

San Josef Bay
Holberg
Kains Lake
Port Hardy
Beaver Harbour

Fort Rupert (Tsaxis)
Sointula
Malcolm Island

Coal Harbour
Blackfish
Sound

Pulteney Point

Rupert Inlet
Port McNeill

NORTH

Port Alice
Alert Bay

Beaver Harbour

0   kilometres   24

Introduction

PORT HARDY ON NORTHERN VANCOUVER ISLAND was nothing but a one-horse town when I grew up there in the 1950s and 1960s, except that there wasn't even a horse. There was a herd of cows though, belonging to the Holmgren family who lived on the flats at the estuary of the Quatse River, but those cows spent more time in the village shaking bottles out of the cardboard beer cases in people's sheds to eat them than they did grazing on the flats.

What no one knew when my family first moved there in 1953 was that the Port Hardy I would grow up in would develop at the same time from a sleepy little logging village into a thriving town with three booming industries by 1975.

Various mining attempts in the immediate area since the 1800s had not turned into anything significant; one logging company harvested most of the wood, and though a handful of men had commercial fishboats, the fishing industry had not changed much since the 1920s. Along with the drone of seaplanes landing and taking off and the squawk of seagulls and crows squabbling on the shore, the *putt-putt-putt* of the single-cylinder fishboat engines was part of the soundtrack of growing up in Port Hardy.

In the 1950s and 1960s the town wasn't even at the end of the road. There was no road out. The northern part of Vancouver Island was only connected to the rest of the island when the logging roads from the north met the logging roads from the south in 1963. Until then, the town was accessible only by sea and by air, courtesy of the World War II air base built in 1942.

The long-promised highway to Port Hardy was not completed until 1979.

The gravel road from the airport into the village was muddy in the winter and dusty in the summer until a truck from the logging company based near the head of the bay poured oil over it.

Scott's General Store in town was the source of everything from groceries to clothing and hardware. The owner also ran a small commissary in the MacMillan and Bloedel logging camp with loggers' necessities like caulk boots, work pants, Stanfield's sweaters and rain gear.

Growing up there in the 1950s and '60s, us kids were pretty much left to entertain ourselves when we weren't in school, and I was the beneficiary of free-range child rearing.

We would wander up the local rivers, trying to catch trout or harass salmon spawning in fall, dodging black bears who were doing the same thing. We would run around in the woods, cutting trees down and building cabins we never finished, or row out in the bay with legitimately acquired or "borrowed" rowboats.

My father was an energetic French Canadian with roots going back to the first settlers in New France in 1634. He enthusiastically embraced life on the BC coast after arriving to work on the log booms in 1947. He wasn't really an outwardly demonstrative person; he showed his love and affection in his actions. He included me from an early age in everything he did off the job and, as soon as I was big enough, on the job too. He took me fishing, first recreationally and then commercially, firewood cutting, shake-block collecting, hunting and even to the town's two bootleggers on occasion.

The beach was our playground when we were kids. In this 1959 picture I am six, my brother Marc two and my sister Louise almost four. *Marcel Drouin photo*

My family lived in several different houses that were built adjacent to the beach in Port Hardy, all between Fisherman's Wharf and the log dump where my father worked on the boom. One was only half on land, with the other half on pilings over the shore so that at high tide the water came in under the house. On windy days driftwood logs would get washed up to the house and bash against the posts holding the house up. My mother, who was already frightened of the water, said that one of the most terrifying moments of her life was when she looked out the window of the house at high tide one day and saw all three of her children seated on a log and paddling out to sea. That would have been when I was about eight, my sister Louise six and my brother Marc four years old.

Free-range child rearing indeed. Once we were out the door, we were free to do what we liked.

We would spend endless hours on the beach in front of the house following the tide as it receded, turning over rocks to find tiny crabs, bullheads and eels underneath them. On extremely low tides green and purple sea anemones appeared at the water's edge, which the older kids warned us to never step on because they were "blood-suckers" that sucked your blood right through your gumboot.

I set myself on fire once. I was trying to get a fire going in the yard and it just wouldn't catch, so I threw some gas on it, spilling more on myself than on the fire. My whole front from my knees up to my chest burst into flame. I ran for the beach, and fortunately the tide was in, and I jumped in the water, extinguishing the flames, but not before I lost my eyebrows.

They couldn't keep us away from sharp tools and guns. I split my knee open with a hatchet one time; luckily I didn't permanently cripple myself by cutting deeper into the kneecap. When we were building one of our "cabins," my friend Clifford whacked me in the web between my thumb and forefinger with an axe. Another time, we were having a BB gun duel and he shot me between the eyes. One inch either way and I'd have been blind in one eye.

Seafood played a big role in our lives in those days. Canned coho salmon was a staple. We regularly ate crabs, as my father brought them home from the log boom where he worked, or I caught them with a homemade bicycle-rim hoop trap off the floats at Fisherman's Wharf. I could never figure out why I could sell the crabs to American tourists on sailboats for a dollar when all they had to do was throw a trap over the side themselves. In winter, when the tide went all the way out in the bay, we'd go dig clams by the bucketload in the rich beds at the low-water line. Never mind that we all lived right on the shore with raw sewage from the houses going right out into the sea to be washed over the clam beds with the tide. Fecal coliforms were something only lab rats in universities knew about; we sure didn't.

A lot of people burned wood, and the scent of wood smoke was always hanging in the air along with the salty tang of the nearby ocean. If you got anywhere near the log booms or even along a logging road when a logging truck passed, the fragrance of freshly cut logs and bruised bark filled the air.

I got into a bit of bother with the law for a brief period in my early adolescence and ended up getting sent away to Montreal for a year. That took me away from the rut I was afraid life in Port Hardy was leading me toward and opened up my eyes to other possibilities in life than being a logger. After meeting a collective of university students who were putting together an alternative newspaper, I realized these included writing.

I started my writing career in high school when, in the autumn of 1968, the North Island Gazette contacted North Island Secondary School, looking for a high school correspondent. I got the job, which wasn't very difficult as I was the only applicant. I wrote a weekly column from the high school until I graduated in June 1971. It was mostly about regular school news, basketball scores, bake sales, sock hops and such events, though I did write a lengthy feature about our field trip to Expo 1970 in Osaka, Japan. I didn't mention in the article that I got caught in the bunk with Hilary from Campbell River and nearly got sent home.

When I graduated, the editor of the North Island Gazette wanted to hire me as a reporter, but I planned to travel the world, and as the Gazette was offering $1.25 an hour and I could earn $3.90 working on the log boom, it was a no-brainer. After working in the forest and fishing industries, I didn't get into professional journalism until May 1990, when I was hired as assistant editor of the United Fishermen and Allied Workers' Union newspaper, The Fisherman.

I could have written much of this memoir when I was eighteen years old, but I thought that what I had seen growing up was lacklustre and boring. I didn't realize that I was witnessing a transition of lifestyles from the handlogger/gas-boat era to the computer age in my own lifetime.

Now, fifty years later, I realize I am lucky to have seen it close-up.

I hope I'm providing at least a snapshot of a few scenes of life on the coast in those years. We'll never experience that kind of life on the coast again.

1 / A Day Trip to the Islands

WHEN WE WERE KIDS growing up in Port Hardy, people would ask us what we wanted to do when we grew up. Most of us expected to be loggers just like our fathers, or dreamt of one day owning a commercial salmon troller. But now that question suddenly became completely irrelevant. If this rowboat sank, we weren't even going to see our thirteenth birthdays.

No matter how hard I pulled on the oars, I just couldn't make any headway. We were in the middle of Goletas Channel now, halfway between the Gordon Group of islands and the shore of northern Vancouver Island, still miles away from our homes in Port Hardy, tucked in at the head of the bay I was struggling to reach.

The afternoon westerly had come up in the channel, which, combined with the ebbing tide, had made the waves grow into small swells that were getting larger by the minute. If we didn't get across the channel soon, we were going to be in real trouble, getting either swamped by waves or swept farther up the channel between Vancouver Island and the smaller islands of the Gordon Group. If we disappeared completely, no one would ever know what had happened to us, except that Kevin's father's rowboat was missing.

It had been fun so far. The day had started out much more pleasantly.

We hadn't told anyone, but my best friend Kevin and I had been planning this trip for a while.

I still can't remember if we skipped out of school that day or if it was a Saturday, but anyway, after considerable planning, Kevin and I met up as early as we could at his parents' place for our adventure.

First thing we had to do of course was get the guns. When you're a twelve-year-old boy in Port Hardy, you can't go on an adventure without carrying a gun.

I don't know how we got away with it—his dad must have been at work—but somehow we managed to sneak two guns out of his dad's gun cabinet, load up the rowboat at the finger float down in front of the house with our supplies for the day, plus the guns, and depart without anyone catching us.

Port Hardy was mainly a logging town in 1966. A handful of men had commercial trollers but very few of them were full-time fishermen; they worked mainly in the woods and fished in their spare time in the summer during fire season, for example, or when the woods shut down for a strike. My father owned a small troller himself, from 1959 to 1964. The main employer in town was Mac-Millan and Bloedel, which had a big camp, logging operation and booming ground in Port Hardy. My dad had worked for that outfit when it was called the Alice Lake Logging Company when he first came to Port Hardy in 1953.

Kevin's father, Ken, had a small logging company called O'Connor Logging, then working out of a camp up at the mouth of the Nahwitti River on the Vancouver Island shore northwest of Port Hardy, roughly across Goletas Channel from Bull Harbour on Hope Island.

My dad had quit working for M&B and was working on the log boom for O'Connor Logging in Nahwitti at the time. The previous summer, I'd spent a couple weeks at the camp working with him.

Kevin and I were outdoor-type kids who spent all our spare time starting log cabins in the woods, prowling the beach, walking up riverbanks, or out on the water if we could get access to a rowboat. Since my dad had sold his skiff with his troller two years before, I hadn't been able to get out fishing from a boat much like I had when I was nine and ten years old.

We were both familiar with guns too, having already accompanied our fathers hunting deer up the various logging roads that branched out from Port Hardy. Thus we felt the need to be fully armed whenever heading out.

Pretty soon I was seated on the back seat of the Davidson skiff, and Kevin was pulling hard on the oars so that we could get out of the inner harbour unseen. The Davidsons were wonderful rowboats, finely shaped so that they cut through the water, with a keel to keep them going straight as you rowed. Looking behind the boat, I could see whirlpools forming behind us as Kevin stroked away effortlessly on the oars. He was shorter and stockier than me. I'd always been a skinny kid.

We slipped away from the shore and rowed past the point of land where the Ellen Logging log dump had been and where the new cannery was being constructed, went inside the concrete post with the light on it warning mariners of the reef there, through the kelp beds covering the reef and toward our destination, Doyle Island, six miles away on the distant horizon.

After the cannery, there was the Melans' house on the beach, then Kevin's uncle Dave's house up on a ridge over the shore, the Spencers' big yellow house, the Cadwalladers' big Victorian house as well, the Seagate Hotel and the government dock. As we carried on past the dock, we pulled out almost into the middle of the bay, skirting the marker warning mariners of a big sandbar at the mouth of the Tsulquate River. The new houses of the Indian reserve there were the last sign of people.

We carried on, sharing rowing duties, though Kevin was able

to make the smooth fibreglass rowboat go faster than I could. I was skilled, though, having spent many hours with oars in my hands as well. Along the northwest shore of Hardy Bay, the forest came down almost all the way to the ocean, with rocky cliffs at the very edge as the trees ended.

Then, at the very end of Hardy Bay, there was a narrow gap in the landscape as the shallow, kelp-laden passage between Vancouver Island and Duval Island appeared. Duval Island is very small, but Duval Point, the land that pokes out into Goletas Channel, was a key marking point and popular sport-fishing spot.

I remembered when my father had a commercial troller and used to fish very close to the rock bluffs there, streaked orange with iron ore, as the echo of the single-cylinder Easthope motor echoed back at us.

As we left Duval Point, we were suddenly in Goletas Channel, the passageway all the way out along the eastern shore of Vancouver Island to Cape Scott and the Pacific Ocean. Our destination, Doyle Island, the tallest and biggest island in the Gordon Group, was directly across the channel. All we had to do was row the final two and a half miles across.

Fortunately, it was still early in the day and the afternoon westerly hadn't come up yet, so we had an uneventful crossing. Right in the middle of Goletas Channel, though, looking to the northwest, the channel was a straight line all the way to the Pacific Ocean. We were very small out there.

The scent of the sea water seemed even stronger now, with the breeze flowing across the almost glass-flat surface and filling our nostrils with the richness of the salty air. You could almost chew it.

Finally, as we approached the shore of Doyle Island, it appeared to rear up over us like a big green cliff with rocky outcroppings. Then we had to find a place to land the rowboat. There was kind of a cleft in the shoreline right in the middle of the island, so we poked the rowboat into there and beached it on a little section of gravel in between the otherwise solid, rocky shore. We pulled the boat up as far as we could and secured it with the bow rope to a tree. The last thing we needed was for the skiff to drift away on us. Nobody knew we were there, and except for a bare minimum of rations, we had no food with us.

But we had guns. Of course, we had guns. Kevin carried his father's precious double-barrel Browning 12-gauge shotgun, and I got the .30-30 Winchester. We had brought along ammunition, of course, so I loaded the rifle and cocked the lever, jacking a cartridge into the breech and cocking the hammer as I closed the lever. Even though I was only twelve, I knew enough to realize that it was stupid to walk around with a cocked and loaded gun, so I held the hammer with my thumb, pulled the trigger and carefully lowered the hammer. If I needed to shoot, all I had to do was pull it back and cock it again.

I can't remember if we had day packs or what—they certainly weren't common in 1966—but we somehow must have brought something for a full day's trip like that, maybe something in a shoulder bag. But anyway, armed and packed, we set out to explore the island. There was quite a tangle of bush along the shore, but once we shoved our way through it, there were paths or game trails to walk on. What we wanted to do was find a way to climb up to the top of the island.

We had barely started our hike in the bottom of this narrow canyon between the two major portions of Doyle Island when suddenly a deer burst out of the underbrush about fifty yards in front of us, running along the hillside. I raised the Winchester, and with barely enough time to sight on the running deer, I fired at it and missed, the loud report of the rifle echoing back at us in the canyon and making my ears ring. It was still within range, but unfamiliar with lever-action rifles and excited, I just recocked the hammer instead of working the lever to reload, and when I pulled the trigger the rifle just went *click*.

We decided to start climbing then. The island was very steep, and we had to zigzag while finding paths to climb up. It was amazing that deer could live on such a small island, but they probably swam back and forth between Doyle Island and the smaller islands in the Gordon Group.

But soon even the deer trails on the lower part of the island petered out. Maybe there was no need for the deer to climb up, as there was plenty of vegetation for them to eat on the lower part of the island. In any event, soon we had to find our own way up the steep hill.

And it was getting tougher. The higher up we got, the less bush and more rock there was, with very little to hold on to. And when you're carrying a rifle or shotgun in one hand, you only have one hand for pulling yourself up over a rock, while clinging to a skinny little bush with very little holding it to the rock face.

We would scramble across a bare rock face, barely finding handholds, until we reached the next clump of bush and a flat place to rest before seeking out another route uphill. We had done very little rock climbing and route finding before, except for my solo trip along the shore to Duval Island earlier that year.

Here on Doyle Island, we continued our struggle to gain elevation. There was no salal to speak of once we got away from the beach, but up on the hill scraggly spruce trees were trying to hang on, and there were even a few stunted huckleberry bushes, probably brought over by birds from Vancouver Island. Nothing provided a very secure handhold though, so we had to be careful when pulling ourselves up or we'd pull the bush right out of the seagull shit or whatever it was it was rooted in.

Occasionally, I looked down and started to wonder how the heck we would get back down. If route finding on the way up was hard, going down was going to be harder. I got tingly in the knees just looking down, not being very good at heights.

I remembered being terrified of looking down when we climbed the water tower up at the ballpark. Going up was fine if I looked up, but once I pulled myself up onto the deck and then looked down over the railing to the ground below, I started shivering all over. How the hell was I ever going to have the nerve to look down the hole in the deck to grasp the top rungs of the ladder to descend to safety? I was starting to feel like that up here.

But still we kept going and finally, after one last scramble up and across what must have been the biggest, barest rock face yet, we reached the top.

The top of Doyle Island was just a bare boulder with some moss in its cracks. The weather must have been too harsh there for so much of the year that nothing would grow, not even the stunted little spruce trees that clung to the bare rock that we had just climbed.

As usual, it was a cloudy day, but that didn't prevent us from seeing the view. Looking directly across Goletas Channel to the south, we could see Port Hardy, six miles away in the distance. Port Hardy was much smaller then, so at that distance we could barely make out a small scar along the shore that indicated the town was there.

To the north we could follow the shore of Vancouver Island on our left as far as we could see, with Goletas Channel stretching all the way to the open Pacific. Duncan, Hurst and Balaklava islands were on our right, with Nigei Island rising behind them. Looking the other way, to the southeast again, we could see the shore of Vancouver Island on our right, with Beaver Harbour and the airport in plain view, and Malcolm Island in the hazy distance after that.

We imagined that this must have been a lookout for the Haida in the old days, where they watched out for raiding war parties coming from the north.

I think we must have eaten what food we had brought along— probably a can of sardines and some white bread or something. I doubt we had even brought water to drink. Neither of us owned a canteen, and plastic water bottles hadn't been invented yet.

We didn't have a watch with us either, but we knew that we had better get going if we wanted to get back before dark so our parents wouldn't miss us or, worse, realize that we had taken the rowboat without permission. So we started the scramble down.

As I'd feared, going down was harder than going up. Oddly enough, what had seemed like an obvious route up from below was obscured on the way down, so we had to carefully pick our way, holding on to our precious guns the whole time with one hand, of course.

Finally, we made it back to the beach. Thankfully, our rope had held the skiff securely. We stowed everything back in the boat, dragged it down the gravel and rocks to the water and launched it, settling into our seats as the boat bobbed out from the rocky shore of the island. Seeing as Kevin had rowed most of the way over, I volunteered to row back, or at least start rowing back. At first it was easy, while we were still in the lee of the nearby islands, which were blocking the northwest wind that was starting to come up in the channel. It was starting to whip up the water too, at first in ripples, but soon in small waves. I pulled on the oars and rowed us farther out into the channel.

It was harder to row than usual, but I was determined to do my share. But as I approached the middle of Goletas Channel, I realized that no matter how hard I pulled on the oars, I wasn't making any headway at all. The combination of the wind and the tide had us at a virtual standstill. Plus, the waves were getting bigger as the wind picked up, lapping at the sides of the boat so that we were starting to get little splashes of water into the boat.

Kevin noticed that we weren't getting anywhere too and finally said, "Let me row, you come back here," and we swapped positions.

Kevin was stronger than me, and once seated behind the oars, he got the feel of the boat in the water and started pulling forcefully, struggling against the wind and the tide, but starting to gain some headway across the channel. More than I was achieving anyway. It still seemed a long way to Duval Point, though, which I could see clearly on the other side of the channel, over his shoulder.

But even though we weren't perceptibly closer with each pull of the oars, Duval Island and our safe homes in the distance somehow got closer and closer. Good thing too, because by now the wind had really come up and whitecaps were starting to form as the waves got bigger and bigger, with the skiff rising and falling on the swells formed under the waves.

A grim look on his face, Kevin kept up his strong pulling on the oars until finally we rounded Duval Point at the entrance to Hardy Bay and got out of the worst of the wind and the waves.

Once we got into sheltered waters, I offered to take over the oars again, but Kevin just shook his head and kept pulling us closer and closer to town. As we approached, I could more clearly make out the thin line of houses along the beach and the government warehouse at the end of the government dock where the weekly steamboat arrived with groceries and other goods for the town.

Pretty soon, we cruised by the Tsulquate Reserve, and shortly after that past the end of the government dock, the Cadwallader house, the Spencers', Kevin's uncle's ranch-style house up on the hill, the Melans' and the new cannery, and around the corner and along the shore to the little finger float, where we pulled up in front of Kevin's house.

After successfully completing our adventure without mishap, we were quickly unloading the boat onto the float when things suddenly went sideways.

I successfully got the .30-30 Winchester out of the boat and onto the boards of the little walkway, but somehow as Kevin was stepping off with his father's precious 12-gauge Browning double-barrel shotgun, it slipped out of his hands and dropped between the float and boat and into the water and plunged to the bottom.

Years later, I forgot completely about this sad conclusion to our trip to Doyle Island, but I was reminded of it by Kevin's brother Daryl when we met at his uncle David's memorial in Vancouver.

I might have helped get the other stuff in the house. Somehow, we managed not to attract any attention, but the shotgun was still at the bottom under the rowboat.

I must have scurried home to avoid the fireworks, but apparently Uncle David came and saved the day. Daryl told me that, in tears, Kevin told David what had happened, and after they retrieved the shotgun David took it home, took it all apart, oiled it and reassembled it and replaced it in Kevin's dad's gun locker without ever informing him. Uncle David had the utmost respect of his nephews after that.

Kevin's father's family, the O'Connors, and his mother's, the Gundarsens, were considered "old-time" families in Port Hardy, with roots going back decades, but in 1966 my family were relative newcomers, having arrived only in 1953.

2 / **Port Hardy, 1953**

WITH NO ROAD IN OR OUT, like a lot of other logging towns on the coast, Port Hardy in 1953 was served by the Union Steamship line, whose boats dropped freight off on their weekly trips up and down the coast. Unlike most other communities on the coast, though, Port Hardy boasted a wartime-built airport.

Nearby Coal Harbour also benefited from the air force when the Western Whaling Company bought the site and buildings of the air force's seaplane base there, built in wartime to patrol the nearby Pacific Ocean. The site came with hangars with big bay doors, docks, accommodation and a huge, sloped ramp designed to pull seaplanes out of the water, perfect for processing whales.

The whaling station opened in 1948 and ran until 1967.

Port Hardy's biggest industry at the time was logging, centred on the camp owned by the Alice Lake Logging Company division of the Powell River Company. There were some small-time "gyppo" loggers and a handful of fishermen, but industrial-scale logging was the mainstay of the village.

That's how my father got there in 1953. After coming to BC in 1947 from Quebec, where he'd worked the log drives, he worked on the boom in camps all along the coast. He'd gone back to Montreal in 1952, married his childhood sweetheart, my mother Rita, and convinced her to move to BC.

My father then worked on the log booms up in the Queen Charlotte Islands (called Haida Gwaii now) but he quit that job and was flying home to Vancouver, where my mother was living with baby me in Richmond in a small rented house. My mom always called it Lulu Island, because that is the island that Richmond is on, but I guess in those days they called it Lulu Island as often as they called it Richmond.

My dad was a typical logger at the time: get a job in a camp, work there for three months, quit, come to town, take a break and then hire out on another job in another camp. With a wife and a newborn son in Vancouver, though, he was eager to find a place to settle down. In those days there was no direct flight from the Queen Charlottes to Vancouver, so they flew in stages, from Queen Charlotte City to Port Hardy, then from Port Hardy to Vancouver.

During the stop in Port Hardy, he and the other loggers on the plane took a taxi into town and stayed overnight in the hotel. My dad must have had a good look at the town on the way in, because the road ran along the edge of the bay, past the big log dump and booming ground and the houses along the shore, and then up the hill and into the core of the village, which wasn't much more than a store and two hotels at the time, with a population of around eight hundred.

After the night in the hotel, they caught the taxi heading back to the airport for the second leg of their journey. As they drove by the logging camp, the taxi driver turned to them and said, "You guys are loggers—want to stop in and see if there's any work going? We've got plenty of time before the plane leaves."

They agreed and my dad went in and talked to the superintendent, Bert Holbrook, asking if there was work. Yes, there was.

"How many days a week?" he asked.

"We work eight days a week here," Holbrook replied.

My dad mentioned that he had a wife and child in town and noticed quite a few houses there in Port Hardy—did the company have any accommodation for families? Yes, they did, he was told, if he wanted to stay. So he did. The rent was $10 a month and $3.50 for electricity.

As soon as he got settled, he called my mom in Richmond and told her to pack up all their things and the baby and take the Union steamship to Port Hardy.

So she did exactly that. Although terrified of the water, barely able to speak English, and carrying a five-month-old babe in her arms, in October of 1953 my mom boarded the Union steamship *Catala* for Port Hardy. I don't know how my mom had the nerve to get on the boat.

I can't imagine what she was thinking as the boat left Vancouver's harbour, steamed under the Lions Gate Bridge, and crossed the Strait of Georgia, heading for the channels and straits between Vancouver Island and the mainland on the way north to Port Hardy.

Steamship day in Port Hardy: the whole town came down to the government wharf to see who was arriving, who was leaving and what freight was being unloaded. Sometimes someone's new car even came ashore in a sling carefully lifted off the deck of the boat and gingerly landed on the dock.

My dad would have been waiting when the boat came in, I'm sure. He would have been twenty-eight years old, my mom twenty-five. Me, five months. It was October 30, 1953. I can just imagine my mother at the gangplank, carrying me, I imagine the luggage would have been unloaded by a sling and sorted on the dock.

They had both been pretty snappy dressers before I was born, so I'll bet she had her best clothes on and I'll bet my dad looked his best too, freshly shaven, lined up at the dock with all the other expectant people waiting for loved ones. I'll bet that after sorting

My mother and me at the little white company house on the shore my parents rented for $10.00 a month plus $3.50 for electricity. *Jules Drouin photo*

the luggage and offering a quick greeting (he wasn't one for public shows of affection), he piled her and me into the car and drove the mile to the little house they were renting from the company.

I don't remember it, of course, but I have seen plenty of photographs. It was a cute little white-painted house, a two-room cottage really, perched on the shore of Hardy Bay facing where the Fisherman's Wharf is now. If there was a wharf at all—and I don't recall seeing one or much of one in the earliest photos of me on the beach—it wasn't much more than a single finger for a handful of boats to tie up to. It expanded over the years, particularly after they dredged the basin in that corner of the bay.

What did she think when he led her into the house? Or even when they parked on the road outside?

Her life had gone through a lot of changes since she left home.

She had come from small-town Quebec, left home to get away from her oppressive father, lived for a few years in Montreal and

worked for Holt Renfrew, sewing fur coats. Then my father came
back from the West Coast, married her and talked her into moving
to BC. That was a huge step for her, moving all the way across the
country, not knowing a word of English.

She got a job at Mount Saint Joseph Hospital in Vancouver,
a francophone hospital at the time, and worked there until she was
too pregnant to work. I was born there.

Now, after a two-day boat trip with an infant in her arms, here
she was in Port Hardy. And my dad had got them their first real
home together.

I think they were burning wood in that first place. The next
couple of houses we lived in had fuel-oil stoves, but in some of the
earliest photos that my mom took, particularly of my dad and me
with a deer he had shot, the deer is hung in a woodshed next to a
neatly cut and stacked pile of wood. My dad was always fond of
cutting wood.

I don't know if he was doing it right away in 1953, but in later
years, when we had a bigger house farther along the beach toward
the Glen Lyon River bridge, and he was still working on the boom
for M&B, they'd let him use the boom boat at lunchtime to take a
deadhead fir home and shove it up on the beach at high tide. After
work he'd secure it with a rope, and on the weekend or when he had
time he'd cut and split and pile it in the woodshed. I spent many
boring hours during long summer evenings helping him do that
when I wanted to be off with my friends, enjoying the longer days.
But that was later...

I think they were happy. My mother was probably still very
much in love with my dad at the time. There is a handful of photographs that are still around somewhere of those early years. I
recall one she took of him walking home from work. The booming
ground, where they made giant log rafts to float to mills down
south, was only a short walk down the road, and of course she
could see where he was working from the beach in front of the

house. In this photo he's wearing his stagged pants, cut off at boot-top level so they wouldn't get wet in the water when he was working on logs, a wool mackinaw jacket, probably a plain grey one (he didn't like the checkered ones, I remember), and a canvas "Bone Dry" hat that he wore to keep the rain off. I think he probably has a cigarette going too.

They had a little Kodak box camera and often didn't get close enough to whoever they were photographing, but in this case she got close enough, and you can even see the pleased expression on his face because he was getting home to his warm house, his wife and son.

As I grew up, my mom took various pictures of me, sometimes with my father, sometimes alone. There is one I recall quite clearly, having seen it so many times. It is me at about age three, standing in my dad's little rowboat that he used to go out fishing in the bay. He would sometimes take me along, and I remember him telling me that I learned to walk on logs because as soon as I could toddle, he took me out to his little boat that he had moored at the end of the logs at the boom where he worked. He'd take me out there, put me on the logs and have me walk out ahead of him to the boat, following closely behind in case I lost my balance and fell into the water. And as far as I know, I never did fall in.

There are several other photos that I remember clearly too. There is one of me and our dog, a cocker spaniel called Skipper, and another of my dad dressed in his clean weekend at-home clothes and little me at two or so on the Quatse River bridge. I don't know if they walked all the way out there; I doubt it, they probably had a car by then. My dad always liked to have a car.

I don't know if my father had done much deer hunting when he was in Quebec. I know that he had a single-shot 12-gauge shotgun that he said he had wounded a deer with because all he'd had with him at the time was birdshot, so he'd had to club it to death, and that's why the butt stock was broken.

Once he got settled in Port Hardy, he noticed that there were plenty of deer around if you went looking in the newly grown-over clear-cuts that started right on the outskirts of Port Hardy, past the logging camp marshalling yard, and stretched far into the hills where the logging had already taken place and the shrubs and baby trees and alders and fireweed were coming back.

Without a deer rifle, he figured he could just buy a box of slugs and use the shotgun. He went to the store one day and asked if he could get some slugs for deer hunting. What he didn't know was that it was illegal at the time in BC to hunt with slugs. Or at least that is what he was told by one of the old-time locals who happened to be hanging around the store because he didn't have anything better to do.

"You can't hunt deer with slugs, that's against the law," this guy almost yelled in my dad's face. He still remembered that fifty years later.

My dad went hunting and shot a deer and had it hanging in the woodshed when, guess what, the game warden showed up, accompanied by another one of the long-time residents of Port Hardy, one who fancied himself an unofficial assistant to the game warden, kind of a non-deputized stool pigeon, you might say.

"So, I heard you shot a deer, Jules," the game warden said to my dad. Obviously, he'd been told by the guy with him and maybe others that my dad had been looking for slugs for his shotgun.

My dad said that yes indeed, he had shot a deer, and of course the game warden wanted to look at it.

"So, what did you shoot it with, Jules?" the warden asked.

"With a .303—you want to see the bullet hole?" my father offered and parted the hair on the buck's chest and showed the hole from a .303 bullet, smaller than a man's little finger, not the big, almost-one-inch hole that would have been there had he used a slug.

"Oh, you've got a .303?"

My dad explained that a fellow down the road had just sold him one the week before.

So the disappointed local guy, who thought he'd show off and help the game warden charge the new-in-town French Canadian guy with illegal hunting, left with his friend the game warden, having made a lifelong enemy out of my dad.

"I hate his guts," he told me fifty years later when the man in question lay dying in a hospital bed down the hall from where he was after a stroke.

I wish I had that rifle now, but my father loaned it to an alcoholic friend of his and we never saw it again. It was a very nice Lee-Enfield sporting rifle with proper hunting front and rear sights, not the original, crude military ones. I'll never know if it was a converted military rifle, but if it was, it was a very good conversion. But it was possibly a sporting rifle to start with. I still remember the way the stock almost glowed with a reddish tint. I wouldn't be surprised if it had been made with rosewood.

There is a picture of my dad and a deer with that rifle. Funny, though—in the photo the barrel on that gun looks a lot longer than the barrel on the one I remember from when I was twelve and finally permitted to shoot it.

There is another photo of my father and me with a deer hanging up in the woodshed. I'm two years old and holding on to one antler while he's holding the other and propping up the head of the deer for the photo.

I don't really remember those incidents, except for the fact that I have seen the photos. What I do remember, and this is perhaps one of my earliest memories, is that outside Scott's General Store I saw some very big grown-up boys in uniforms with funny little caps on their heads and scarves around their necks, selling apples. It wasn't until years later that the Boy Scouts formed a "troop" in Port Hardy, and I started to see these little boys in Cub Scout uniforms and realized that those big grown-up boys

I had seen years before were in fact Cub Scouts. So I must have been little.

I also remember being out alone on the road in front of the house and seeing a house on fire on the other side of the road. But the whole time I was growing up after that, I never saw a site where there could possibly have been a house, so that is a strange but persistent memory.

Perhaps the most traumatic experience of my life, though, was when my family was visiting a section of Port Hardy known as "Stagger Alley," which was anything north of the corner that marked the centre of town, where the road made a T and turned left to a street where Tex Lyon lived or turned right and went down past Charlie Lynch's restaurant/pool hall and the upper hotel.

I couldn't have been more than four or five and was outside trying to play with the older boys, which was a bad idea considering the nature of those boys, a tough bunch. But anyway, there I was.

There was a hole in the ground that they had covered up with a board or piece of plywood or something and they were taking turns going in one end and out the other, like a rabbit or dog searching for rats or something. That looked like fun, and someone encouraged me to climb in. I eagerly did, and once I was down in the hole, they covered up the exit. There I was, trapped inside in the cold and dark and trying to get out, crying and maybe hammering on the board while they stood above the plank laughing and jeering, I suppose, I don't know. I also don't know how long I was in there, but finally someone opened the hole and let me out. Maybe my mother cottoned on to what was going on and noticed I was missing from wherever they were visiting and realized they had me trapped in the hole.

I have been claustrophobic ever since.

3 / **Grade One**

AFTER THE SUMMER WHEN I WAS SIX, I had to start school. Gone were the days when I was free to do anything I wanted. Even when I was five years old, my mom let me out of the house to go wander around on the road or down on the beach where I mostly played, turning over rocks at low tide, looking for tiny crabs and bullheads.

I went fishing for a week with my father on his small commercial salmon troller, and then suddenly it was September and I had to go to school.

The air was already thick with the smoke from slash fires. They still burned slash fires on the logging clear-cuts in those days, to burn off the treetops and branches in an attempt to clear the land for second-growth trees to be planted. My earliest memories of September are filled with the scent of the smoke that filled the air at that time.

There was no kindergarten in Port Hardy, and parents (at least mine) in those days were not interested in teaching kids the alphabet or encouraging them to learn their numbers. That's what school was for.

I had only a passing acquaintance with other children before I started school. I knew Vicki Reilly, the girl next door, and we played together, but I hardly knew any other kids. The first day of school was a huge event, my very first exposure to being in a large group and having to pay attention and be obedient to that degree.

I didn't know much about what school was before I started either. I remember I saw some very grown-up children walking by toward town and asked my mother where they were all going at the same time, and she probably replied in French, which my parents spoke at home, "À l'école," and that was it. I was exposed to English outside the house, and my parents spoke more and more English at home, so by the time I reached school age, I was bilingual.

I guess I had a fair notion of what the school was because we had to go by the building perched at the top of the hill past Fisherman's Wharf on the way to Scott's General Store in town.

My mother must have taken me to school that very first day, and I remember that for the next eight years of my schooling, I walked up those wide steps to the main entrance in two flights, with a small deck in between and a carving of the two-headed serpent Sisiutl over the top of the stairs, where the hallway started.

I don't think I had ever been in such a large building. The Port Hardy community hall was big, but it was really just one large room.

That first day of school, I was exposed to a tidal wave of experiences. For one thing, Robert Scott School had students from grades one to twelve, so we were suddenly sharing the hallways with high school students who were as big and mature-looking as the teachers. At first, I couldn't tell who was a teacher and who was a student. My grade one teacher had only a couple of years' experience teaching at that point and was in her early twenties, while some of the older high school students were eighteen or nineteen. For another thing, even though I knew a handful of other kids in Port Hardy, suddenly I was in a class with thirty-five others.

I don't remember much about the very first day of school except that our teacher introduced herself as Mrs. Toth, and the smell of plasticine and freshly sharpened pencils as she prepared us to learn the alphabet.

Then Gladys Moore peed in the sandbox. I didn't know about her family at the time, but once I was in school, I got to know her two brothers, Bobby and Jimmy, and occasionally played with them. I don't think they had a toilet in their house, just an outhouse, so when she had to pee, Gladys didn't know what to do and just hoisted her skirt and let fly in the sandbox. I don't remember much else, but I'm sure she was mortified at the reaction of the teacher and the other little girls.

I took to reading pretty quickly, apparently. Fifty-two years later, on the day after my father died, I went to the seniors' home where he had passed away to make arrangements with the funeral director and ran into Mrs. Toth, visiting the mother of an elementary school friend.

"Oh, Michel, I was just talking about you the other day," she told me, after passing on her condolences.

"Really?" I asked, puzzled. Why in the world would she be talking about me so many years later?

"Yes," she said. I'm sure Mrs. Toth never said "yeah" in her life. "I was just talking to someone the other day about your grade-one class," she explained. "I remember I was reading a book to the students, and I had to leave the room for some reason, so I called you up to continue reading the story."

Well, I didn't recall that at all, but it was very flattering to hear her say that. I knew I picked up reading quickly and devoured everything I could find once I had learned to read, but I didn't know I could read out loud to a class before I had even finished my first year in school.

There wasn't a lot of reading material around the house. My mother subscribed to a trashy monthly magazine called *True Story* that had scandalous stories in there about teen pregnancies, extramarital affairs and other adult goings-on I had no clue about, of course, but read anyway. She also had a subscription to an equally trashy Montreal crime-reporting newspaper called *Allo Police*, which had stories about bank robbers, grocery store holdups and gangland murders, including grisly photos of dead shooting victims and automobile crash casualties. And this was in French, of course, which I was not studying at all, only hearing around the house, so as I learned to read English, I was teaching myself to read French at the same time.

The other exciting thing about going to school was, of course, meeting all the other kids in the school that I had had no previous contact with. Most of their fathers worked for the logging company like my dad did, but there was one boy in my class whose dad did something at the airport. I found out many years later that he was the meteorologist there.

Kevin O'Connor was the first student I immediately connected with. Kevin's father had his own successful logging company, whereas most of the fathers of the rest of the students were employees of M&B, the main employer in Port Hardy. Kevin's dad, Ken, and his uncle David drove around in red Mercury pickup trucks with "O'Connor Logging" emblazoned on the side.

Along with the main logging company in Port Hardy, MacMillan and Bloedel, there were a lot of small "gyppo" logging operations, independent outfits ranging from tiny one- or two-man logging businesses with minimal equipment to larger enterprises, with float camps, bunkhouses and logging trucks. Some did better than others, and O'Connor Logging seemed to be the most successful.

When the rest of us kids were lucky enough to get a Slinky or an Etch A Sketch for Christmas, the O'Connor kids all got new bicycles. Kevin had two younger brothers and a sister.

Kevin's uncle Dave, who was known as "Pogo" to his friends, had a huge Chesapeake Bay retriever called Simba that he told us kids was half-cougar. Kevin's family lived in a large, brand-new home along the shore adjacent to Fisherman's Wharf, and seeing as my family lived not too far along the road past Fisherman's Wharf, it was inevitable that we would end up playing together. Besides, we both liked hanging around down at the wharf, particularly on Einar Johnson's old boat the *Canadac*.

Einar was a crusty old handlogger/fisherman who seemed to like having kids around, or at least was tolerant of them. He never seemed to be able to remember our names or didn't care to learn them. He always called Kevin "the Irishman's kid" and me "Pea Soup's kid."

Kevin hung around Einar so much that his family took to calling him "Kevin Johnson."

He'd let us pump his boat out. The *Canadac* had a big old deck pump that looked like a big iron bucket with a big piece of iron in the middle to slip the end of the long pump handle into. You had to pour a bucket of water into the top and start pumping the long handle up and down until it started to suck the water up from the bilge. That grey water was the most foul-smelling stuff you could imagine, smelling like sulphur, farts, rotten mud and shit all together. I can't imagine how the bilge water could ever get so foul-smelling, as that boat hadn't had any fish on board down in the hold for about thirty years at least—but it sure got your attention.

Kevin was the one kid I spent the most time with because we lived so close to each other, but I got to know everyone else in my class too, some more than others.

Among them were the First Nations kids. Even though there was the large Kwakiutl community of Fort Rupert out toward the airport, the Indigenous and white population didn't really mix very much. Some of the men from Fort Rupert worked in the woods, and those who did were always very good loggers. My dad had a few First Nations acquaintances he worked with on the boom, and I even remember one or two coming over to the house on occasion. But for the most part, the whites and First Nations rarely associated, so it was a revelation to suddenly be in a classroom with some of the kids from Fort Rupert.

There were two brothers, Buster and Freddie, that I am still friends with years later. Their older brother Andy was in the class ahead of us and I got to know him too. I became friends with a boy named David too. He was quieter than the Wilsons, paid more attention in school and usually did well.

I'd already experienced some prejudice and harassment from other kids in Port Hardy for being French Canadian, and also for not being part of the extended family of the first white settlers there, but I never got that feeling from the First Nations kids.

They were different from the white kids—funny and practical jokers, but athletic and competitive too, and could usually outdo the white kids in running and rope climbing and other sports. They weren't afraid to fight too, if challenged. Even at six or seven, they would never back down from a challenge to fight.

They smelled different too, if you got close to them, which you can't help but do in elementary school. The Wilson kids, at least. They must have heated their home with wood, because they always smelled of smoke. Either that or they had smoked fish in their sandwiches, which was probably true as well. But most likely they had the same thing as the rest of us: Spam on white bread with bright yellow baby-shit mustard on top.

Most of the other kids lived either at the airport or past the centre of town, where I didn't usually hang around. We got to know each other and even invited each other to birthday parties, but I never felt close to any of them.

A few years later, when I was older and got a bicycle, I would ride the eight-mile gravel road all the way out to the airport to hang out with the airport kids, or go to Fort Rupert to hang out with my friends there.

I got to know Bruce Nicholson from across the bay too. He lived with his parents and older sister Diane in a house with no road access, and Diane, who was only two or three years older than us, would run their little gas boat from their house to Fisherman's Wharf, where we would meet them for the walk up the hill to the school.

We didn't get to hang out with Bruce very much though, because of where he lived, but I think before the school year was out he invited a bunch of us over to his house for a birthday party, and I remember his dad ferrying a whole boatload of us six-year-olds across to the other side of the bay in the little gas boat.

It was only a few years later that O'Connor Logging built a road around to the other side of the bay, past Bruce and Diane's house, for a log dump and booming ground. Then I used to regularly ride my bike over to hang out with Bruce and go on adventures farther along the shore past the log dump.

4 / Bill's Bomb

BEFORE I STARTED SCHOOL and moved into my elementary school years, I used to wander up and down the beach in front of our house, exploring the shore. Several houses past our place, toward the log dump and booming ground where my dad worked, there was a boathouse jutting out over the beach at the mouth of the Glen Lyon River.

That was Bill and Kathy Scotton's place. Approached from the road, their place was different than any other home in Port Hardy, notably because of the giant maple tree in the yard in front of the big old house.

They did all kinds of interesting things. The house had a rich, smoky scent inside from the beach-stone-faced fireplace, with a wire-mesh popcorn maker on a long handle hanging beside it that I never got the chance to see in action. They also had a well-established garden and even a compost box, something I never saw anybody else employ until the mid-'70s.

Kathy died in her early fifties, I think, but not before doing stuff with me that I remember well. I was a curious, nosy little kid and loved hanging around with Bill and Kathy when my father wasn't home.

We lived along the beach, next to the road that ran from the logging camp and the airport into town. Bill and Kathy's house was virtually on the banks of the Glen Lyon River; then along the shore toward town there was another full-size house, then a small house, then us, another two or three houses, then a stretch of bush and Fisherman's Wharf.

Bill and Kathy's place was the best, though. Their garden was so productive because the ground had been worked for a number of years, and also because it was established right on an old First Nations midden, and they fertilized it with compost, seaweed and fish scraps.

I don't remember much about Kathy except that, most likely because her own grown son and the grandchildren were a long way's away in Terrace or somewhere, she probably missed having kids around and put up with me.

I already had a fascination with guns even at the age of seven, and noticed this very unusual little gun in their gun rack one time and asked about it. It had no trigger, and even then I understood firearms required triggers to discharge them.

I remember I showed so much interest that Kathy took the gun from the rack and took me out along the river, out to the low-tide mark, and demonstrated how the gun worked.

The beach in front of their house was bordered by the channel of the Glen Lyon River. At low tide you could walk for hundreds of yards along the river.

She worked the bolt like one on a normal bolt-action rifle, opening it and leaving the chamber open, then slipping a .22 cartridge into the breech and closing the bolt.

The gun had a little sliding push button on the top of the pistol-grip, and she aimed at a crow or something and fired by pushing the button forward with her thumb. The rifle went off with a little crack. That was my introduction to .22 shooting.

I guess Bill was already retired, as I don't remember him ever going to work.

Bill was very fond of steelhead fishing, and his preparations for the winter-run steelhead started in the summer when he saved salmon roe from salmon that he had caught. He made a mixture of brown sugar, salt and borax and laid the brown paste and roe in small wooden boxes until they were full and sealed them. The brown sugar, salt and borax preserved the eggs until he needed them; then he made little pouches of the prepared eggs with nylon stockings.

I asked him where he got the nylon stockings, and he said you had to chase a lady up a tree and pull her stockings off.

Bill had a boathouse and had built a troller called the *Kathleen* there.

I think the *Kathleen* had been recently completed, or some other boat had, because the inside of the shed was fragrant with wood shavings.

The whole boatshed was a wonderful storehouse of fascinating things for me. Just outside the entrance it had a wonderful, mysterious device that always caught my attention even though I never saw it in action.

The boatshed was built out over the high tide line, so that at high tide, the water lapped at the end on pilings. The other end was built resting on dry land.

There was a wooden-plank walkway down from the edge of the garden to the shed, and just before you entered the shed through a solid wooden door, there was this strange-looking kettle-type thing built out of a forty-five-gallon oil drum on a stand, with pipes coming out the top so that a fire could be built underneath it.

The pipes led into a long black tube about a foot and a half around, an old wooden culvert made out of strips of wood, just like a barrel, coated with tar and held together with steel bands.

It was a plank steamer. The tube was fixed in place at about my height, and at the other end a flap of old inner tube kept the steam from coming out.

When building a boat or replacing a plank, workers would cut a piece of wood to fit the shape they needed for the hole they were filling, then fire up the boiler and insert the plank into the old culvert. After a certain time, the plank would be so malleable from the steam that they could take it into the boathouse and fit it to the frame of a new boat or into the slot where an old or broken plank had been removed from an existing boat.

And that was before you even went into the boatshed. The door was a large, heavy wooden one made from planks, like the rest of the building. I can't remember if it had a latch or not, but it was kept shut by strips of rubber inner tube nailed to the inside.

Once you were inside the boatshed, it was first a pleasant assault on the nostrils. There was the scent of yellow-cedar shavings, a unique odour that you can't really describe. It's bright and spicy, tangy and sweet at the same time. No other wood smells like it. Then there was the odour of copper paint for the bottoms of boats, top paint, and other paints, creosote for preserving the boatshed itself or ribs and planks inside the boat, plus the scent of other kinds of wood chips and shavings.

There were pieces of wood sitting on the exposed beach bottom, and when the tide came in they didn't float. I asked Bill what kind of wood that was and he said, "Iron wood." I couldn't imagine how a tree could grow iron.

What fascinated me more than anything else, though, was a wall of cubbyholes built like twelve-inch-square boxes. Each one had a different pile of stuff in it.

Every hole was built into the wall and attached to the next by a small shelf along the front of it, so that things wouldn't fall out and you could reach in and select exactly what you wanted.

Different sizes of long bolts with their accompanying washers and nuts, different pieces of unidentifiable brass fittings, nails and screws, were in each box.

One day I was shuffling through one box, and sitting there on the bottom was a big, rounded, cylindrical object that I couldn't identify. I removed some pieces of metal that were on top of it and saw that it had fins on the end.

It was cold, and heavy. It was all I could do to pick it up and carry it over to Bill, who was busy shaping a plank to go into the boat he was repairing.

"Hey Bill, look what I found," I announced proudly.

Bill, who was a skinny, pale, white-haired man, went even paler.

"Where'd you get that?' he asked firmly, dropping whatever he was doing and walking deliberately toward me until he was close enough to touch me.

"Over there," I said, indicating the cubbyholes.

"Give me that," he said, reaching out and gingerly taking it from me.

Without saying another word, he walked straight to the door of the boatshed, out the door, through the garden, past the house and onto the road. I tagged along as we walked right by my house until we came to Fisherman's Wharf. We walked out to the end of the airplane float, the longest finger at the wharf, where the seaplanes came in, and he threw the mortar bomb out as far as he could.

It made a big splash and disappeared. It must have been a relic left over from the Pacific Coast Militia Rangers, a volunteer civilian defence organization in World War II. There was also an old Canadian army helmet hanging on the boatshed wall.

Bill was a cool guy. When I was delivering newspapers and he was widowed and living on his boat, I sold him an occasional paper.

In the summer, Bill worked as a fisheries guardian for the Department of Fisheries and Oceans. Fisheries guardians were private contractors who provided their own vessels and patrolled parts of the coast for the fisheries department where it couldn't have full-time fisheries officers on duty. The guardians mostly maintained a presence to prevent illegal fishing, but also monitored fisheries as they occurred.

Later, when I was eighteen years old and had a serious travelling bug, I came back from a six-month trip across Africa, worked for a while, saved a little bit more money and headed off for South America. I never made it, but my first destination in Mexico was Mazatlán, in February 1973. Bill was living down there, by then in his retirement years, with a woman and her two children. He called her his "housekeeper" but everybody who knew him thought otherwise.

I just showed up at his door and he took me downtown to a cheap hotel. The funny thing was that somebody else from Port Hardy was in the same hotel, Chris Sondrup, an older man from across the bay, so we ended up hanging around together for a few days until I got my feet under me.

I ended up sleeping in a hammock in a beach hut a little north of town, at a trailer park that had kind of a walled compound, so we were safe from robbers. I stayed there until I decided to move on to Mexico City. I never saw Bill again, but after I met my future wife in Japan later that year, I brought her to Port Hardy and introduced her to Chris.

5 / Gary Ewart

GARY EWART AND HIS YOUNG WIFE Jeannie lived in one of the other houses that were lined up on the shore between Fisherman's Wharf and the Glen Lyon River.

There was a big empty space between our house and the next one, which wasn't much more than a cabin, really. Cole Graham lived in this small house before Gary and Jeannie moved in. I remember he was a kind of cool, Marlon Brando type of guy who wore a leather jacket and rode a motorcycle. He took me on a ride once, and I remember clinging to him as the engine roared and everything beside us sped by like crazy.

Cole also built a car in the space between his house and the beach. At least to me, as a small child, it looked like he was building a car. It was a mould he had fabricated out of chicken wire and papier mâché to make a fibreglass body for a sports car based on a Ford Cobra, I believe. I didn't know that at the time and all I could do was wonder how in the world he could make a real car out of wire and newspaper. He got much of the papier mâché done, but then it rained on it and I think he abandoned the project.

Cole moved into town around that time anyway and Gary and

Jeannie moved in. I think it was their first home together.

When Gary first showed up in Port Hardy in the early 1960s, he made an immediate impression with his passing resemblance to James Dean and his Elvis hairstyle.

When everyone else was driving boring-looking family cars from the 1940s and even older beater pickup trucks, Gary drove a bright-red 1952 MG TD convertible sports car. All the teenage girls in town couldn't keep their eyes off Gary, and all the young guys envied his car.

He started dating the town beauty. I still remember them lying together on her parents' lawn romancing when I was about nine or ten, maybe. She couldn't have been more than fifteen and he was maybe eighteen or nineteen. She was cute. Even as a ten-year-old kid, I knew a pretty face when I saw one. What was amazing was that she had such delicate features, as her parents were both large and plain with coarse features.

Things moved fast after that. Next thing you know, they were married when Jeannie was still only sixteen years old.

Gary was kind of a phenomenon. No matter what he turned his hand to, he was good at it. He must have started out in the woods as a chokerman, but before long he was a hooktender, basically the boss of the sidehill.

He used to go hunting with my dad and me, and I was impressed because he had a Savage lever-action rifle while my dad still hunted with an old Lee-Enfield .303. My dad had a rowboat hidden in the woods at the edge of Kains Lake; we'd take it across the lake to the meadows on the other side, where there was an old log cabin on the shore.

I remember we were resting at the cabin after hunting one morning, and Gary came back carrying some antlers. At first, we thought he was dragging a deer, but it was just the skeletal head of a two-point buck.

He and Jeannie lived for a while in the small house and then, after their first child was born, moved into a bigger house next door. I remember babysitting for them after they moved.

One thing I remember well is the bearskin. In those days nobody in Port Hardy shot bears to eat. They were considered just big rats or racoons that you saw at the dump. But one day Gary was out deer hunting and saw this big bear and decided to shoot it for the hide. He skinned it and tacked the hide flesh side out onto the old garage wall that was close to the road beside his house. We could see that hide every time we went outside. It was huge and reached almost all the way from the eaves of the shed to the ground. I still remember the smell of the thing. It had its own smell that is hard to describe—musty and animal-y, but not foul. At least not at first.

I think Gary must have made some effort to scrape some fat and flesh off it, because you could see the texture of the hide; it was pockmarked with dots, the way pigskin is if you see it preserved.

But that hide never dried on that garage wall the way Gary hoped. The climate is so damp in Port Hardy that it rotted, and he threw it on the beach for the crabs and seagulls. But that kind of thing happened there. It was rare that anyone kept a trophy of anything, though I knew that there was a mounted mountain-goat head and deer head on the wall in the beer parlour of the "lower" hotel in Port Hardy. I knew that because I used to stand up on the railing and peer through the ventilator fan hole at the heads, yellowed from years of tobacco smoke in the place. Rumour had it that they were local legend Einar Johnson's.

Preserving animal hides and heads to show off was just not something people did in Port Hardy. They shot animals to eat or for public safety. My father shot a large cougar right on the street in the mid-1950s when people complained it was persistently hanging around. He paraded around town with it tied to the hood of his car for two days, then threw the carcass in the dump. He shot another cougar in the 1970s when he came home from work and my mom said her dog Winner the cockapoo had been having a standoff with a cougar all afternoon. It was just a cub, but he shot it and then got in hot water with the conservation officer over it. That got dumped too.

It wasn't until I was nine or ten and visiting a friend's house where his dad had a "den" that I first saw a tanned animal hide. It was a raccoon skin.

Gary had this idea of starting a boat rental business, but he had no boats. He started building them in his father-in-law's old garage across the road from their house. I used to drop in and see what he was doing all the time.

He bought some basic pre-made fibreglass hulls of boats. They would have been fifteen or sixteen feet long. The hulls were thin and floppy, so he had to construct the whole interior of the boats. So, when I went to see him, he was either cutting up pieces of plywood to make bulwarks, filling in the keels with wood, or making floors and seats and fibreglassing them in place. The eye-watering, nostril-burning odour of fibreglass resin filled the confines of the small shed. The whole time he was doing this, he had to make bases for the engine in each boat and plan where the driveshaft, shaft bearings and stuffing box would go through the stern. He also had to fashion a simple steering mechanism. If I remember right, it was with an external rudder controlled by someone sitting in the back seat.

When the first one was complete, it was a beautiful thing, glossy and white on the outside, with the finished interior including a Briggs & Stratton motor smack dab in the middle of the deck.

Gary built some extra floats and got permission to attach them to Fisherman's Wharf, along with a small shed for the office. As he produced these boats, he launched them and tied them up at his dock. They were fun to use, with just the Briggs & Stratton motor that started with a pull cord and a simple gearbox. He didn't charge very much per hour and even us kids could rent one and take it out.

Some older teenagers rented one and took off and didn't return that night, causing concern for the whole town and panic for their parents until they were spotted stranded on a beach out in Goletas Channel.

The business looked like it was going to be a going concern, particularly in the summer if tourists showed up, even though we still didn't have a road to Port Hardy at that time. If people wanted to come to Port Hardy, they had to take the coastal freight boat from Vancouver or fly.

Gary also partnered with my friend Clifford's father, Walter Manson, and started a Honda motorcycle dealership. Honda had just started importing motorcycles into Canada, and Gary was on it like a cat on a mouse. Pretty soon many of the young loggers and other young men with disposable income in Port Hardy were scooting around on sleek Honda 65 bikes.

By this time, he and Jeannie had three kids.

Then, one day in the fall of 1965, I came home from school and my mom said, "Gary Ewart was killed today."

From what I understand, Gary was in the landing, where the logs were piled after being pulling downhill. They had loaded a logging truck, but one log had somehow ended up crossways. They decided to trip the bunks—the upright struts holding the timber on the truck bed—and then unload the truck and start over. They hooked up a D4 Caterpillar to the trip lever on the truck bunks, and for some unexplained reason Gary walked right under the load as they tripped them, and he was killed by the logs as they rolled off the truck.

Accidents happened a lot in the woods in those days. Guys would get killed by a log if it got pulled off the hill while they were not in the clear, or a cable would snap and cut a guy in half as it whipped around.

Now Jeannie, who was barely twenty years old, if that, was suddenly a widow with three kids.

Gary Ewart's active personal and business life was cut short by a logging accident.
Rolf Leben photo

The death of Gary Ewart hit the whole community really hard. Everyone felt terribly bad for Jeannie and the kids, of course, but it was also a reminder that that kind of thing could happen to any of the men working in the woods. It was only a few years later, shortly after they started the Boy Scout troop in Port Hardy, that one of my scoutmasters was killed in a logging accident. One of the yarder operators died when a cable broke and one end whipped into the cab and killed him. One of my dad's friends lost his leg when a log crushed it.

But Gary's death had a cascading effect on Port Hardy. His business ventures changed hands, and not too long after he died Jeannie took up with a prominent member of the community, which had a profound effect on all the families involved.

Who knows? If he had lived, with his drive and developing entrepreneurial skills and Port Hardy growing bigger, as it was about to, Gary would probably have become one of the town's more successful businessmen.

Gary's death put an end to my babysitting, so I ended up becoming the paper boy for the area.

6 / M&B Camp

WHEN WE WERE LIVING on the stretch of road between the
M&B log dump and the Glen Lyon River, one of the Masterman boys
from up the road past the dump delivered the *Vancouver Sun*. First it
was Norman, and then Tommy, who was a couple of years older than
me. Their father was the timekeeper at the M&B camp and also the
first-aid man. I knew that because my dad took me up to the camp
to see him when I whacked myself on the knee with a hatchet while
playing in the yard and trying to get a fire going. He patched me up
as best he could. I still have a significant scar on that knee.

I remember Tommy lugging the huge sack of newspapers by
the house for years. Funny, despite being a voracious reader as a
kid, I'm not sure if my parents took the paper. I think they took the
Sunday paper, which was the biggest of the week and contained
my favourite reading at the time, the *Star Weekly*, a magazine full
of stories from across the country. It was from the *Toronto Star* but
included in a syndication by the *Vancouver Sun*.

It wasn't long after Gary Ewart got killed in the fall of 1965
that either Tommy himself or Mrs. Ross, who was the agent at the
airport for the *Sun*, approached me or called the house. I remember

Tommy having lots of money to spend on chocolate bars at May's Café, and I had really no other opportunity to earn any kind of money at all, so I eagerly jumped at the chance, ignoring the fact that most of the time I would be lugging a heavy canvas sack laden with newspapers along the road. I suppose that one reason Mrs. Ross thought of me was that I was right in the middle of the route. Most of the subscribers were near our house, either along the road to the southeast of us, up the hill at the ballpark, or at the massive M&B logging camp. The rest of the subscribers were to the northeast along the road, past the wharf and down into the little area we called Bush's Plantation because that is where the Bush family lived with houses on both sides of them and then along the shore. My grade two schoolteacher, Mrs. Eckley, and her husband and my friend Kevin's family were along the shore there.

So I agreed and took on the route. The routine was that Mr. Deans, who drove the passenger bus from the airport after the five o'clock Pacific Western Airlines flight arrived from Vancouver, dropped off my bundle of papers in front of the house. It was a tight bundle, held together by two strong copper-coloured, square-cornered wires that took a pair of cutters or pliers with a cutting function to open. I had to retrieve the papers right away when he dropped them off because it usually rained in Port Hardy, particularly in the fall, and I didn't want to deliver wet papers to anyone. I got them under cover and counted them out so that I had the right amount to carry in each direction. The bulk of them went in the direction of the logging camp and the ballpark, so that was where I went first. I had so many that I had to put them in two bags and carry one over each shoulder. Fortunately, I had a shortcut up the hill toward the ballpark near the house in the form of an old Cat road. It was overgrown with alders by then, but there was a trail through it used by the schoolkids from the ballpark, so I used that path.

The ballpark was a wide, flat area that had once been the site of a World War II air force hospital that moved to Alert Bay in 1947.

I had a whole round of *Vancouver Sun* subscribers at the ball-park. It was basically a gravel road with a row of houses on each side, and just about everyone took the paper, so I was able to get rid of about a dozen papers there. After the ballpark, I followed the road down the hill to the M&B logging camp.

I was quite familiar with the camp, as from the time I was very young my dad used to take me to the camp every few months for a haircut. There was a man there named Matt who was a long-time employee who cut hair in the evenings. It was in one of the original eight-man bunkhouses, with a large central room and a big oil furnace there heating the whole building. In each corner of the long building was a room with two bunks in it. The wall opposite the door was lined with coat hooks where the men hung their wet gear up to dry after work.

The first thing you noticed on entering these bunkhouses was the odour. It was a combination of sweat, sawdust, power-saw gas, cigarette smoke, snuff and aftershave that hung in a thick fug in the air.

I remember Matt's electric clippers. He would cut hair with scissors and then finish off the back of the neck and along the sides of my head with electric clippers that heated up and burned when he touched the back of my neck. I was really grateful to the Beatles, because after I saw them on TV on *The Ed Sullivan Show* on February 9, 1964, I avoided getting my hair cut.

The smell hadn't changed when I started delivering newspapers to the bunkhouses in camp.

M&B was doing very well out of Port Hardy at the time, and they had expanded the bunkhouse camp for 150 men with some new accommodation. They still had the old-fashioned, classic bunkhouse style with a main room and four bedrooms, but there was also a long, almost motel-style bunkhouse, now with individual rooms. That building was a single structure with a covered porch running the whole length of it, and rows of individual rooms lined up one after the other.

There was one even newer building that was more like a two-storey apartment building. I delivered newspapers to them all. While the rooms were different, there was one thing in common. They were clean.

The "bull cooks" at the camp—the cleaners and housekeepers, usually older men who couldn't work in the woods anymore—did an amazing job. They might have been looked down on and even ridiculed for being the "maids" and janitors in camp, but every room was clean and tidy, the beds were made in a rigid military-barrack style and the floors were swept clean, and they did not tolerate messes left lying around either.

The walls over the bunks of many of the younger loggers were covered with centrefolds from *Playboy* and other men's magazines. This was long before explicit photos of women were featured in grittier magazines like *Penthouse* and *Hustler*, so all that was really being exposed were pretty faces, bare breasts and bums. That was enough for me, at age twelve, to get to admire the variety of women on display over each bunk. Most of the older guys were neater and didn't mess up the walls like that.

I was an avid reader, though, and couldn't help but pick up the magazines when I was in the men's rooms, I would start reading whatever books they had lying around their bedside tables in the rooms. That's when I got into real trouble.

One guy had a copy of *Fanny Hill: Memoirs of a Woman of Pleasure*. I think I must have already heard about that book, so I couldn't help myself. I picked it up and started reading. My god! My mom had some weird kind of soft-porn novels around the house, but they really were women's romance novels with only the bare suggestion of sex in them. But this was marvellous. It described the real thing without actually using the real words for genitals, but it was lively and thrilling nonetheless. I would start reading a portion of this copy of *Fanny Hill* and time would stand still for me, and I had to shake myself out of a reverie to get out of the room and carry on my paper route.

After I discovered that guy's *Fanny Hill*, it became a daily exercise to read a portion, until one day there was a note on the bed: "To whom it may concern," it stated, "personal items and reading matter are private property and must not be touched." I'll never know if that message was meant for me or the bull cooks, but it sure embarrassed me, and I made sure to be quick and efficient and just toss the newspaper on the bed and get out of there from then on.

***

The logging camp where I delivered the newspapers had been a fixture in Port Hardy since the 1940s.

Logging had been under way for years by the time my father came to Port Hardy to work for Alice Lake Logging in 1953.

A company called Spicer Logging had started working in the area in 1939, and then sold out to Alice Lake Logging, a subsidiary of the Powell River Company, which started logging in the Alice Lake and Port Hardy areas in the 1940s.

The Powell River Company and MacMillan and Bloedel merged in 1960, and this became the Port Hardy division until the company moved to Port McNeill in 1974.

The years when I was growing up were the glory years for the Port Hardy division.

From 1967 to 1969, for example, an average of seventy loads a day were being dumped into the water in Port Hardy, with crews working day and night shifts.

With the logging occurring farther away from Port Hardy and closer to Port McNeill in the early 1970s, M&B decided to move all operations and their 235 jobs to Port McNeill.

M&B may have left Port Hardy, but O'Connor Logging remained. O'Connor Logging was one of many smaller, family-based logging companies in Port Hardy, working at the same time as M&B and its predecessor, Alice Lake Logging, but on small timber claims that they could get along the shore of Vancouver

Island, on local islands like Nigei Island, or up in the mainland inlets like Seymour Inlet. Curley Hope, O'Connor Logging, Melan Logging, Lemon Point Logging, Storey Logging, Ellen Logging, Eilertsen and Carlson Logging were among them.

Some did better than others, and O'Connor Logging seemed to be the most successful. Ken O'Connor had started with partners Billy Scotton (son of Bill Scotton) and Dave Jackson on logging claims on Nigei Island. O'Connor bought his partners out in 1952. His brother David joined the company in 1961.

O'Connor took over the Eilertsen claim at the Nahwitti River and eventually built a substantial camp on the flats adjacent to the estuary of the Quatse River, at the head of Hardy Bay. The company had logging claims up the new logging road going to Holberg and built a road around to the other side of the bay, where they established a log dump and booming ground.

That road opened up a whole new world of exploration for me, offering the opportunity to visit places that had previously required a boat to get to, and I hadn't had a rowboat since my dad sold his with his troller in early 1965.

7 / **Chris Across the Bay**

WHEN O'CONNOR LOGGING BUILT THE ROAD around to the other side of the bay, past my friend Bruce Nicholson's house, it provided access to several abandoned houses and sheds there, as well as solitary bachelor Chris Sondrup's once-isolated home. That's when my real exploring across the bay got started.

Long before the road was built, Sondrup lived over there in a neat little house that he had built slightly up the hill from the shore. He had a sawmill there too, but I don't remember ever hearing or seeing it in operation. Even as kids, though, we heard that it was powered by a straight-eight Packard engine. I'd always been curious about the house next to Chris's, an abandoned place with only the peak of the roof and a small portion of the house showing above a thick tangle of salmonberry bushes.

Chris wasn't a friend of my father's, so I didn't get to know him until much later.

When we were kids, we'd see him row across the bay in his tiny skiff, rowing in the old-fashioned pushing style. I thought this was weird because I always rowed in the pulling style for fishing, which allowed me to watch my fishing rod off the stern of my dad's rowboat. The benefit of the pushing style, of course, is that you can see where you are going.

As children, we didn't know his last name, so we called him "Chris across the bay." I wouldn't say that he was unfriendly, but he was a very private individual and most likely just didn't have time for kids, so we didn't get to know him in the same way we got to know Einar Johnson, who lived on his boat at Fisherman's Wharf and enjoyed having kids around.

We would see Chris walk slowly from Fisherman's Wharf and along the road, up the hill and back down into town to go shopping at the store. I don't know why he didn't row directly from his place over to the government dock. Maybe he enjoyed the short boat trip and the walk to town. He always carried a small canvas backpack to bring his groceries back down to the wharf and home again by boat.

Chris was from Denmark and had moved to the Cape Scott area at twenty-two in 1925, after the collapse of the Cape Scott Danish settlement experiment. Danish immigrants had attempted to settle near Cape Scott in 1897, but harsh conditions forced the collapse of the original settlement in 1909. Another wave of Danes arrived later and settled at the San Josef River valley, near present-day Holberg. In an article in the *North Island Gazette* in December 1980, Chris explained that he initially took over a homestead on the Cape Scott Trail but ended up giving it up and moving into Holberg. He settled in Port Hardy in 1947. My friend John Lyon was very close to Chris. Chris was a mentor to him, encouraging him to seek higher education mostly because of his limited vision. John told me that Chris was the first one to take him to Vancouver for an actual eye exam by an eye specialist. I guess John was one kid that Chris took an interest in, because Chris knew John's father well, and John was obviously a very bright boy.

He even showed John how to build a boat.

I got to know Chris much better later in life, after we had coincidentally met in Mazatlán, Mexico, in early 1973.

Two years later, after more travelling, I was back in Port Hardy with my new German-born wife, whom I had met in Japan in December 1973. She did not like Port Hardy but loved plants and gardens, so I took her across the bay to meet Chris. He was very kind and gentlemanly, and they immediately took to each other. I remember that the first time he made us tea, he poured a small portion into his teacup and sampled it before serving us. While we were there, he took a book off the shelf and showed it to us. It was *Denison's Ice Road* by Edith Iglauer.

"John Daly was here this summer with his new wife," Chris told us. "She's a writer, this is one of her books."

***

Back when I was a preteen, with the new road across the bay, I could easily cycle over to see Bruce. Sometimes, if Bruce wasn't home or was doing something with his dad, I'd ride past the log dump and boom (where I would eventually get a job and work for several years) and go exploring. There was an abandoned house just past the log dump with a shed full of old fishing gear. What fascinated me the most were the handmade fishing lures I found there.

They were made of articulated pieces of red cedar, starting with a large, painted head about one- and-one-half inches square, connected to another one with a thick staple, then another one and then another, for five or six pieces in total, with a piece of rubber inner tube attached at the end to resemble a tail. The head was roughly painted with eyes and a mouth.

They were nearly twelve inches long and designed to resemble a fish swimming in the water. There were boxes of them. I wish I had taken one and tried it out. I think they were probably ling cod lures meant to be trolled deep, near the bottom. They resembled the articulated plastic-dragon toys you can buy in Chinatown in Vancouver.

Chris's house was a little farther along the shore, past the abandoned house with the fishing gear.

Chris Sondrup (left) was not a drinker, but he was talked into coming for a visit on a sunny April afternoon while my dad and his friends enjoyed a beer outside. *Author's collection*

I didn't know Chris at the time and didn't want to cross his property either, so I would walk along the shore past his house. Well, when I was little, he had an older, ivy-covered house right on the waterfront, but later he built a nice, neat cottage up on the bench above the sawmill, where he had cleared land for a substantial garden. The sawmill was perched on the shore just above the tide line too, and I could see that there were still piles of sawdust along the steel guideway and the big old eight-cylinder Packard.

Just past Chris's house, I could see the peak of the house choked in a high tangle of salmonberry bushes. In an old postcard showing the road near Fisherman's Wharf, you can just see one side of it and the roof sticking out of the salmonberries.

I asked my father about the place and all he told me was that it used to belong to someone known as the "Silent Swede." I found out years later that his name was Eric Hedberg, and he was called by that nickname because he spoke so quietly that people could barely hear him.

Once past the sawmill and Chris's house, I would make my way up off the beach into the thicket of salmonberry bushes.

On one occasion, I pushed my way through the spiny salmonberry stems to the crumbling steps of the house, and after carefully climbing them so that I wouldn't go through the rotten parts, I got up on the equally rotten porch and pushed the closed door open.

The first thing I noticed on entering the place, besides the fact that it was completely dry, was that the floor was littered with empty two-gallon tins labelled "Methyl Hydrate."

I can't imagine that Hedberg drank the stuff. I've heard of "rubbies" who mixed rubbing alcohol with water and drank it, but the number of tins there indicated that he must have used it for something else. Maybe an alcohol-burning camp stove or something.

There were stacks of magazines and catalogues inside the place too, and I would eventually spend hours there reading *Look*, *Life* and *Picture Post* magazines from 1948 to about 1952. They were big magazines with lots of pictures. I was already an avid reader by the age of ten, so I absorbed everything in there even though the news articles were over fifteen years old, featuring new movie actors who were either forgotten or huge stars by now. There were articles and photo essays on current affairs as well. I clearly remember seeing a feature about the rebuilding going on in postwar Germany.

Equally fascinating were the mail-order catalogues from those years, with big-tired, big-framed bicycles and leather jackets for kids my age on the pages, as well as the fashions for all ages. They looked old-fashioned and quaint to me already.

Of course, I always looked to see what kind of guns they were selling too, because I hoped to have one of my own one day, and liked looking at them in catalogues, even if they were fifteen years old. I was amazed at how cheap they were.

I didn't pay too much attention to other parts of the catalogues the first time I went there, when I was about ten, but when

I was twelve the pictures of women's underwear were suddenly a lot more interesting than they had been a couple years earlier.

But it was the hummingbirds around the house that struck me the most. As the house was surrounded by salmonberry bushes so high that you could barely see out the windows, the bright pink berry flowers in the spring attracted the little birds.

They must have somehow got in the house and could not get out. All the windowsills in the house all the way around were heaped with the mummified carcasses of hummingbirds, their tiny bodies still glinting purple and green as they lay there piled one on top of the other by the dozen.

I was almost tempted to break some windows in the house to make an exit for them, but at the same time I felt awkward snooping around there in the first place and I had no intention of wrecking anything, even though it was obvious no one was ever coming back to this place.

I never learned anything else about Mr. Hedberg the "Silent Swede," and oddly enough, years later when I got to be friends with Chris, I never asked him about his neighbour.

Around the corner from Chris's place and along the rough, rocky shore, there was a small sand and mostly clamshell beach that Bruce and his sister Diane showed me that we called "Bead Beach," because if we dug into the crushed clamshells there, part of an old midden, we would find trade beads. They were mostly hexagon-shaped blue beads, but there were occasionally tiny red ones with a white liner. We used to call them "Indian beads" because we didn't know any better. We somehow imagined that they had originated with the First Nations people who had lived there long before us. In fact, they were made in Europe, mostly in Venice, though some were from Bohemia.

There were the remains of a few buildings along the shore, mostly inside Jensen Cove, though we didn't know the real name of the place; we just called it "Sole Cove" because that was all we ever caught there. What we didn't know as kids was, that was the original site of the village of Port Hardy, which had been a busy little spot before the town was moved across the bay. All we knew was that there were a handful of ruins there. There were still a few rusty cans and broken bottles to be found around the crumbling scraps of wood that were slowly becoming part of the forest again.

David O'Connor used to tell a story that there were so many beads on the beach there because they were still washing up many years after a First Nations woman dumped a sack of them off the wharf in old Port Hardy to demonstrate how rich she was.

A little farther out toward Queen Charlotte Strait was a big bay we called "Deep Bay," even though its real name is Bear Cove. There was a World War II airplane crash site just uphill from Bear Cove, but there was no trail to it that I knew of, and that is one thing that we had kind of heard rumours about but never pursued. It was a long way away by rowboat, and once we had rowed out that far to fish, all we wanted to do was make it back home before our parents found out we'd gone out that far from the inner bay.

There is a terminal there now for the ferry to Prince Rupert, but when we were kids, nothing was there except some second growth near the shore where the original trees had been logged. What we didn't know was that this was evidence of the earliest site of human habitation on Vancouver Island. Boy, if we had known that, we would have dug there. Who knows what we would have found?

8 / Middens

ALMOST ALL OF THE SHORE around the inner part of Hardy Bay was one huge midden. It was obvious that when you dug into crushed clamshell it was evidence of previous human habitation, only we didn't realize how old it was.

Excavations in 1978 at the Bear Cove site found evidence of human habitation in charcoal samples dating back eight thousand years.

In a research paper, archaeologist Catherine C. Carlson reported that pebble tools, projectile points, bone points, harpoon points, needles and miscellaneous bone artifacts, bone awls and chisels, were all found at the site.

Carlson wrote that she found evidence of twenty-six species of fish, eleven of land mammals, six of marine mammals, twenty-two of birds and twenty-three of shellfish at the site.

We knew of middens, though as kids we didn't know they were called middens. What I remember is that people liked to go dig the "clamshell dirt" (as we called it) for their gardens from places where it was cropping out, because everyone knew that that soil was incredibly fertile.

There was a place I remember clearly right beside the Glen Lyon River when I was growing up. If I had been a little more aware, I might have taken a shovel and dug into it for artifacts.

As it turned out, both sides of the mouth of that river were rich midden ground. After Bill Scotton moved out of his big old house just on the edge of the Glen Lyon River, the Mansons bought it.

When the Mansons moved there, I gravitated toward the place because they had a houseful of boys, and Clifford, the second youngest, was my age, so I would go hang around there a lot. They introduced me to the board game Monopoly, which I had never seen.

One day in 1966 I went over to the Manson house, where they were digging out under the wooden foundation of the house to put in a full basement. They said, "Look what we found under there," and showed me a human skull Clifford had dug up.

He and his younger brother Sam had been digging when they uncovered what they thought was a clamshell at first, then a rock. Clifford struck it with the shovel blade, and when it cracked open they realized it was a human skull. It was fully intact, with teeth in upper part of the mouth. It was stained a dark, nutty brown, like a hazelnut. Seeing as they didn't have to dig any deeper, they did not disturb the rest of the skeleton.

Clifford told me many years later that when Bill Scotton had been putting in pilings under the house, he had dug up three skeletons.

When I was working on the O'Connor Logging log boom on the other side of the bay, John Clayton the dump man would often go for walks along the shore and find all kinds of artifacts in the crumbling clamshell bank there, particularly after high tides had been working away to erode it.

Archaeologists from Simon Fraser University dug in the area just inland of the bank in the summers of 1971 and 1973. The two digs, directed by Margo Chapman, found evidence of very early human use of the area.

Archaeological digs in 1971 and 1973 found numerous chipped stones and bone harpoon points indicating human occupation at least as far back as 3000 BC. *Michel Drouin photo*

In her 1976 master's thesis, "Archaeological Investigations at the O'Connor Site, Port Hardy, British Columbia," Chapman broke down the original First Nations use of the area into two time periods, Port Hardy I and Port Hardy II.

"The earliest, Port Hardy I," Chapman wrote, "is represented by a poorly developed chipped stone industry with no microblade technology. It is suggested that this component is associated with an early coastal hunting and fishing population."

The second period, Port Hardy II, dated approximately from 2500 to 3000 BC. Chapman found that in the Port Hardy II period there was increased use of bone tools and dependence on marine, freshwater resources and shellfish.

As in the later Bear Cove excavations, numerous artifacts were recovered at the O'Connor site, such as ground slate points and chipped stonecutting tools, polished stone axe or adze heads, bone harpoon points and other bone points. Numerous manufacturing tools were also found at the site, which had been used for carving bone antler and wood.

Chapman noted that according to the archaeological evidence, it wasn't until 1000 BC that the culture began to resemble the "well-known Northwest coast pattern of cultural development." Chapman said later that she was grateful to David O'Connor for his generous support over two field seasons and permission to camp on his land during the dig.

In *Yesterday's Promises: A History of the District of Port Hardy* by David Lewis, printed in 1978, the author mentions that the air force built the runway at the Port Hardy airport in the early 1940s on "an age-old resource—clam shells." He makes no mention that in fact those clamshells the air force utilized were dug up from ancient middens left by First Nations people.

***

Mrs. Eckley and her husband, Harold, lived on a midden.

They lived in a little corner of the bay next to a little stream adjacent to Fisherman's Wharf. Mrs. Eckley had been my grade two teacher, and my friends who lived next door said that Mr. Eckley hated kids, so as a child I had nothing to do with them. I was scared and intimidated by Mrs. Eckley and equally scared of Mr. Eckley. It turned out that if he did indeed hate kids, it was only my friends the O'Connor brothers.

A few years later, I started delivering newspapers and got to see Mr. Eckley quite frequently, and he wasn't a bad old guy at all. He had a big machine shop on his property, but it was basically mothballed the whole time I knew him. Whenever I had a chance to glance in at it from the beach, it looked like it was full of rusty old equipment. I think he had retired from the business and only did a little tinkering on his own. It turned out that he had been a fighter pilot in World War I, so he would have been approximately seventy in 1965.

To demonstrate to my wife that Port Hardy had more attributes than its rough-and-tumble, boom-town beer-parlour culture, I took her to meet Mrs. Eckley.

Mr. Eckley was already long deceased by then, and Mrs. Eckley was lonely and enjoyed company. She also liked to drink cheap rye whisky and smoke cigarettes. We didn't drink much in those days, but my wife was an enthusiastic smoker, so we would sit around talking and going outside and admiring her garden, which happened to be sitting on another clam shell midden.

The Eckleys had dug up numerous artifacts when they were building their house and garden, including large hand-held stone hammers. I remembered seeing that kind of stone hammer before. I think John Clayton had found one too.

I often thought how strange it was that such a valuable tool could have just been left lying around for someone to dig up thousands of years later. I don't know what kind of stone they were made of, but they were unusually heavy. I don't know if they were made on the island or imported from the mainland, where they'd been made of basalt or something.

They looked just like large stone mushrooms with flattened tops. It must have taken an enormous amount of work to chip them out of a solid piece of stone with another stone.

When we used to go see Mrs. Eckley, she had some of the stone artifacts on display. When she was living her last days bedridden in her house, things just seemed to have disappeared somewhere. I remember the last time I went to see her; she was blind but fully cognizant of what was going on around her and wept while I held her hand. That was the last time I saw Mrs. Eckley.

9 / **Fishing**

IF YOU WALKED NORTH along the shore from Mrs. Eckley's, past the O'Connor's house next door and along the beach with the uncut forest on the left, you came to a point of land directly across the entrance to the bay from Chris Sondrup's place. That was where Ellen Logging previously had a log dump and booming ground, and where Seafood Products started building their cannery and fish plant in 1965.

There was access via the former logging road that branched off from the main road to Port Hardy just behind the Bush family's house and went up a slight hill and then down to the ex–log dump. My friend Randy lived on the crest of the hill before it dropped down to the beach. The original Melan family home and John Clayton's family home were near the shore to the west on the town side.

I remember that shortly after the pilings were driven there along the shore for the Seafood Products cannery and fish plant buildings, Randy snuck his father's nine-shot .22 revolver out of the house and we unsuccessfully took potshots at seagulls perched on the pilings.

Seafood Products was originally a small Vancouver company and Don Cruickshank, one of the managers there, convinced the owners that building a fish plant and cannery in Port Hardy was a good idea. Cruickshank came to Port Hardy as production manager for the company. With partners, he later bought the company.

When my father bought his little salmon troller from Einar Johnson in 1958, there was nowhere to get ice or to sell fish in Port Hardy. There were small troll camps dotted around the coast, and seeing as my father did not fish far from home, he got ice and sold fish either at Christie Passage or the floating troll camp anchored out at Bates Pass. There was a substantial fish-buying station in Bull Harbour catering to the West Coast troll fleet that fished out beyond Cape Scott on northern Vancouver Island.

There had been no ice plant or buying station in Port Hardy since the 1940s. When Seafood Products built the cannery and fish plant, not only did the company offer competitive fish prices and services to fishermen, but fishermen based in Port Hardy also had all the services, such as a grocery store, liquor store and gear suppliers, that an isolated floating fish camp did not.

It suddenly changed Port Hardy from a one-industry logging town to a vibrant two-industry town. The salmon cannery and fish plant changed the face of the town forever.

There was suddenly work for women, as well as plenty of summer jobs for students who didn't want to go work in the woods. Some of those summer jobs turned into full-time employment and some people ended up spending their whole working careers at the place.

Before Seafood Products built the cannery, Port Hardy was a minor fishing port with only a handful of local trollers tied up at the dock. An even smaller number were full-time professional trollers, who fished the lengthy April-to-October seasons that were common in the 1950s and 1960s. Many of the boats belonged to men like my father who were also loggers and went fishing in the summertime when the camps shut down for fire season or strikes. My father was one of those when he had a boat from 1958 to 1964.

There were occasionally one or two seiners tied up there too; I remember one called the *Porlier Pass* run by a First Nations man from Fort Rupert.

But right around the time the Seafood Products cannery was built, salmon catches and prices increased and fishing became more than just another way to make a living; in some cases it turned into a way to make a killing.

In the late 1960s there was already concern that the capacity of the fishing industry on the BC coast was larger than the stocks could sustain. Consequently, the Department of Fisheries and Oceans (DFO) started implementing limitation plans, such as a buyback of fishing vessels to reduce the fleet, and eventually area licensing for fishing vessels and separating species privileges into separate licences.

Between 1969 and 1977 there was no restriction on the type of gear (gillnet, seine or troll) that could be used on a salmon-licensed vessel. In 1977 a moratorium on the number of vessels allowed to fish with seine gear was implemented.

One plan that benefited big-boat fishermen, investors and the major fishing companies without reducing fishing capacity at all but in fact increasing it exponentially was the vessel replacement plan.

Originally, the concept was that an existing vessel had to be retired if it was replaced with a new vessel. When it was found that people were building larger vessels to replace the retired ones, DFO introduced size limits based on tonnage. Existing tonnage was considered additive, so that one vessel could replace two or more vessels being retired provided that the total tonnage was not increased.

This reduced the number of vessels, but the capacity of the fleet increased exponentially. In many cases two or three gillnet vessels, many of which were dilapidated rental boats belonging to the fishing companies, were retired to build one seine boat. This reduced the number of boats on the water but increased the fishing power up to ten times greater than the vessels being replaced.

DFO's plan for fleet limitation failed completely. It caused a flurry of modern super-seiners to be built, replacing the old wooden vessels built in the 1920s and 1930s.

Port Hardy benefited as catches increased, and the fishing economy in the fleet and at the cannery boomed. In the late 1970s, the Seafood Products cannery was producing an average annual pack of twenty-five thousand ninety-six-pound cases of canned salmon per season. The cannery had a one-quarter-pound canning line and a one-half-pound line in operation. The year 1978 was extraordinary for sockeye, fishermen and the cannery. Exact numbers for 1978 are unavailable, but in order to deal with higher production numbers the cannery employed the one-half-pound line to get through the added volume of fish.

Coastwide catches of salmon peaked at 107,500 tonnes in 1985, and the total landed value of the commercial salmon fishery reached approximately $410 million in 1988.

Seafood Products was perfectly placed to take advantage of high salmon catches, with the growing local seine fleet and high-liners from Sointula and Alert Bay delivering to the company.

"Seafoods revolutionized the industry," Port Hardy troller John Nicholson said, as quoted in the book *A Dream Come True*, published by the Port Hardy Heritage Society. "You could tie up under the boom and they had a crew that came aboard and unloaded all your fish for you." Not only that, but the crew would also wash out the hatch and scrub the pen boards, he recalled.

Showers were available for fishermen, and the company had a pickup truck for grocery shopping, if required.

In the 1990s, catches declined rapidly, to approximately 17,000 tonnes in 1999, the lowest level in the history of the fishery. The total landed value of the commercial salmon fishery decreased to $55 million in 1998.

The fleet expansion and increased catches and value were a lucrative short-term opportunity for those prepared to be in the thick of it.

One such fisherman/investor was James Walkus from Port Hardy, originally from one of the mainland Kwakwaka'wakw families coerced into moving to Port Hardy in 1964. Closely associated with the Seafood Products cannery, Walkus had started out as a gillnetter when he fixed up an unclaimed boat he found on the beach at fifteen in 1954 and went fishing. Sixty-one years later, he told the *Globe and Mail* newspaper that he made $250 that first week of fishing, so the next week he went and bought another boat, a leaky old gillnetter; he had to pump twice a day to keep it afloat.

Walkus built a one-man, multi-million-dollar fishing empire out of his Port Hardy base, with a fleet at the peak of the boom in the industry of nineteen seine vessels, three gillnetters and a cold storage plant.

As commercial fishing's fortunes declined and salmon aquaculture grew, Walkus converted much of his business to farmed-salmon transportation, building two large salmon transporters, the $9-million, 104-foot, 384-ton *Amarissa Joye* and the $11-million, 107-foot, 391-ton *Geemia Joye*.

Roe herring fishing and processing played a major part in Port Hardy's economy as well. Until the mid-1960s, massive volumes of herring were caught on the BC coast for reduction into low-value products such as fish meal and oil. Stocks collapsed and the fishery was closed in 1967.

Stocks rebounded quickly and a new commercial herring fishery began in 1972 for the roe, which was a valuable commodity in Japan. Much lower numbers of herring were caught in the new fishery, with catches in the 35,000-tonne range annually, compared with 250,000 tonnes in the old reduction fishery. Values skyrocketed and the roe herring fishery became the new gold rush in the industry.

Prices peaked for roe herring in 1979, with value of the landed catch reaching $150 million. From 1982, the value hovered around $40 million annually.

The result of high prices and big catches resulted in another building boom of herring punts for gillnetters and more expansion in the seine fleet as owners had to find ways to spend money to reduce taxes.

Seafood Products' facility was centrally located, relatively close to the Central and West Coast fishing grounds, and in March the whole town exploded into activity, with herring fishermen coming and going and many local people and out-of-towners employed in the plant for roe processing.

By 1985 various areas of the coast, such as the west coast of Vancouver Island, were closed to herring fishing once again because of low biomass numbers. By 1988 herring fishing was closed in Haida Gwaii as well. Herring fishing continued into the next century, but with lower and lower quotas and areas along the coast shut down one by one.

**

The Seafood Products cannery and the big-money years were a long way off in the future when my dad took up commercial fishing. It was more of a passion for fishing than a commercial enterprise, but the fact that it could pay for itself must have been an attraction.

My father had loved salmon fishing from the moment he had an opportunity to get a small boat and get out fishing shortly after moving to Port Hardy in 1953. When he bought the *Seagull* off Einar Johnson in 1959, he took salmon fishing very seriously. Until then, he had had a succession of small boats, starting with a tiny little rowboat. Then I remember a small kind of cabin cruiser with a Wisconsin engine in it that was very loud and gave off a stench of burned oil and exhaust.

I used to sit in the stern of his little skiff while he rowed, trolling around in the bay when the salmon were running. I recall sitting in the back of the boat and watching him work away at the oars, with water dripping from them as he lifted them out of the water and swept them forward for the next stroke.

I used to love looking down and watching the water rush by as he rowed the boat along, and when I looked over the stern of the skiff, I could see little whirlpools created as the boat passed through the water. I was very young at the time, and it was not long before my dad got the little gas boat with an inboard engine and a small cabin over the front. That allowed him to go farther out in Hardy Bay, even if the weather was poor.

Funny, I remember very little about fishing during the day, but I remember clearly coming back after dark and watching the reflection of the town's lights in the water, and even the moon on clear nights.

But I remember things more clearly after he bought the *Seagull*. That's when we used to go out on longer trips, staying overnight on the boat for a week or more. The *Seagull* was a thirty-one-foot double-ender, meaning that it had a pointed stern rather than a squared-off one. It was powered by a one-cylinder Easthope gas engine with a large, heavy flywheel mounted in front of the cylinder. To start it, my father had to put about a teaspoon of white gas into a cup attached to the cylinder, open a valve to let it in, crank the flywheel around until he felt the compression build up in the cylinder, then roll the flywheel over against the compression, hoping that the engine would fire.

If it started, there would be the first *bang* of ignition, and if he was lucky, it would fire again, and again and keep going with the characteristic *put-putt-putt*. If it didn't start first try, then my dad had to repeat the whole process.

He took me out the first year he had the boat and numerous years afterwards.

He mostly fished locally on weekends, out at the Masterman Islands and over to Duval Point, then over to the Gordon Group and back to the Masterman Islands in a triangle, mostly for fish to eat. In the summer, he went out into Bates Pass and fished Roller Bay out as far as Pine Island, but most often he liked to tack along the shore of Nigei Island.

It was 1959 or 1960 when I went on my first overnight trip with my father on the *Seagull*. Instead of heading north to Nigei Island and Bates Pass, where we ended up fishing in 1964, the last year he had the boat, we headed south to go trolling in Blackfish Sound. That sounded scary to me; *blackfish* was the term they used at the time for killer whales, and they were considered the scourge of the sea, dangerous and voracious salmon eaters too.

I remember that after sneaking the boat through the rock-piles on the inside of the Masterman Islands out at the corner of Hardy Bay, my dad turned the boat south and we putted along past Beaver Harbour and the Kwakiutl village at Fort Rupert on the Vancouver Island shore, then cruised past the Port Hardy airport, built on a stretch of flat land near the shore.

From the water you can easily see why the area was selected for an airport, as there is a long, flat stretch of lowland along the shore immediately after Thomas Point, a rocky bluff between the airport and Fort Rupert.

Pretty soon we were passing by Pulteney Point, the lighthouse on the northernmost end of Malcolm Island. Port McNeill appeared on our right and on the left, along the shore of Malcolm Island, the village of Sointula.

"What's that place, Daddy?" I asked as we slowly crept by, driven by the slow but reliable Easthope engine.

"Oh, that's Sointula," he said. "There's nothing but Finns there. Nobody else goes there."

After cruising between Malcolm Island and Haddington Island in the middle of Broughton Strait, the next island hove into view and suddenly we were entering a long-curved bay with houses and other buildings all along the shore.

"What's this place?" I asked, noticing that my dad was pointing the boat in toward the other boats tied up at the wharf.

"That's Alert Bay," he said. I don't know why he stopped there—probably to top up the fuel tanks, I guess.

We went ashore too, and I think that was the first time I saw all the totem poles at the graveyard. While we were walking there, we ran into Bill Scotton, a white-haired gent who was our neighbour a couple doors down. I felt like I knew him closely, as I used to go over there and hang around him at his boathouse.

"Hi, Bill," I said.

My dad got pissed off at me. "You call him Mr. Scotton," he said, admonishing me.

"Oh, that's okay Jules," Bill said, laughing. "We know each other quite well."

When we were finished whatever it was my dad wanted to do uptown, we went back to the boat. He turned the flywheel over, got the old Easthope going, and we took off again for Blackfish Sound.

To be honest, all I remember about that trip is the trip. I think the fishing wasn't what he had expected, even though he had mentioned to me that the year before had been the biggest fishing year ever in BC. That was for sockeye, though, and trollers weren't catching sockeye yet. If they were, it was a closely guarded secret, because it was several years before sockeye fishing became a thing for trollers.

Anyway, pretty soon we were back in Port Hardy and back home, and it was a little while before we made another trip, this time out to Roller Bay, hoping to cash in on schools of pinks and coho that were coming through that time of year.

The next long fishing trip that I remember may have been later that year or the next year, but this time we went north.

It was always exciting getting ready to go on a fishing trip with my dad. Packing groceries wasn't very sophisticated, though; he might pack a small bag of potatoes, a loaf of bread, some margarine, mustard, canned corned beef, chuckwagon stew and maybe some cans of spaghetti. I remember eating lots of corned beef sandwiches with bright yellow mustard. Occasionally, my dad would boil up a jack spring with potatoes for dinner too.

Then it was time to get down to the boat, take the tin can off the top of the exhaust pipe, fire up the old Easthope, untie the lines and take off.

Once away from the dock in Port Hardy, my dad squeezed the boat between the shore and the marker mounted on a prominent rock at the entrance to the harbour and pointed the boat toward Duval Point on the northwest corner of Hardy Bay.

Once out into Goletas Channel, my dad took the boat across so that we were skirting the chain of islands that lie off Vancouver Island on the other side of the channel. The first one, opposite Duval Point, is Doyle Island, also the largest and tallest of the group, followed in succession by numerous other little islands. In a few years, my friend Kevin and I would row out to Doyle Island.

After Doyle Island, we cruised by Duncan and Blyth islands, Bell Island, then the shore of Hurst Island. This is where my dad showed me how to steer a boat by marking a point ahead, the top of an island or a headland for example, and then trying to keep the bow of boat pointed in that direction.

Because I had never steered anything before except a tricycle, the boat veered wildly off course at first, and my dad had to come and correct the steering before I got the hang of it and realized that you barely had to turn the little steering wheel at all when you wanted to make an adjustment. It's a challenge for a six-year-old.

Travelling on an old wooden boat powered by a single-cylinder gas engine doesn't get you anywhere fast. The shoreline of the adjacent islands sometimes appears to barely move at all as you poke along.

I always enjoyed looking at the shoreline, even though it was mostly steep and rocky and then choked with trees right down to the water line; occasionally, a little cove or beach would appear, with piles of driftwood logs piled up there. I always wondered what it would be like to go ashore, but if I was on my dad's boat, we hardly ever went ashore.

Once we had passed the Hurst Island shore, my dad took over again and turned the boat into Christie Passage, a wide channel that goes between Hurst Island to its southeast and Balaklava Island on the northwest side. About halfway up the channel, there were suddenly some buildings and fuel tanks tucked into a little cove, and my dad turned the boat in there.

Even before we tied up, I was impressed with all the writing on the cliffs on the north side of the cove. I couldn't read yet, as I wouldn't be starting school until the next month, so I asked my dad what was written there. It was names, dates and boat names, he said.

My dad guided the old *Seagull* up to the float, briefly put it in reverse to stop it and rushed out to tie it up. A man came out of one of the sheds on the other side of the float to see what my dad wanted. There was a scale on the dock to weigh fish that fishermen delivered and an ice machine. He sold fuel too, so I think that is why my dad dropped in. As well as the ice house and fish-buying station on the float, there was a fish storage shed adjacent to the ice machine, and up a long boardwalk onto dry land there was the small store where he sold fishing gear and basic iron rations. His name was Pete McWilliam, and he ran the fish-buying station for the ABC Packing Company.

The place is now known as God's Pocket and there is a sport-diving resort there now, but back in the day we just called it Christie Pass. BC painter E.J. Hughes painted the spot in 1962.

I think we might have stayed the night there, because my dad's anchor stayed piled on the forward deck on top of a coil of rope and he never used it. I complained about that occasionally when I saw other boats anchored up, but now I realize that he would have had to pull it up by hand if he had chucked it overboard. Something else I realize now is that it was just a halibut fishing anchor anyway and might not have held the boat even if it had been deployed. So he preferred to tie up to something and we did, usually a float at a fish camp or at least a stiff-leg log fixed to the shore somewhere.

My dad must have taken some ice from Pete. I don't know what the deal was, whether you paid for it or were expected to deliver to him if you took ice, but even though the side lockers weren't very big and my dad never fished long enough to put fish down in the hold, I remember him putting enough ice in there to be able to keep fish for a few days.

The next day we were up early and putted out of the harbour into Christie Passage, heading out into Queen Charlotte Strait. First, we had to go past Scarlett Point on the northeast corner of Balaklava Island. Scarlett Point was only the second lighthouse I had ever seen, after Pulteney Point on Malcolm Island. Like all the lighthouses on the BC coast, the buildings and keepers' homes were always neatly painted white with red roofs. Scarlett Point's buildings were perched on a nearly bare rock just yards away from the rollers that came crashing ashore from the strait.

Once we were past the lighthouse itself, it was time to get serious about fishing.

Commercial trolling is kind of like glorified sport angling with a lot more lines and hooks. Trollers have long poles on each side of the cabin called trolling poles, which have a complicated array of cables and wires and metal or plastic loops hanging from them. Then the steel cables are swung out away from the side of the boat with these until you have two lines fishing beside the boat, and two more being pulled behind the boat, suspended by Styrofoam and wooden floats called "pigs."

Trollers can have as few as one mechanized spool called a gurdy on each side, or three a side, though some big boats even have four, and each one is fishing about ten lines, so that you can have sixty lines fishing at once. The *Seagull* had two on each side.

First, my dad slowed the Easthope engine down to a very slow rate, going *putt-putt-putt* so slowly that sometimes you wondered if it was going to stall. He pointed the *Seagull* to the northwest, then went out on deck and lowered the trolling poles that were mounted on each side of the mast just behind the cabin.

Each one had a long but strong cedar stick firmly fixed at one end and loose, hanging by a piece of inner tube, at the other, with a bell attached. That was to indicate when fish had struck the lines. Then my dad went to the stern and dropped a cannonball overboard that was attached through a suspended pulley to a steel wire running to the gurdy on the stern of the boat, and started snapping on fishing lines at intervals as he lowered the cannonball deeper into the water.

He had an assortment of fishing lures to choose from, metal spoons that wobbled like a herring, or a flasher and hoochies. The hoochie is an imitation squid, available in a variety of colours. The name comes from hoochie-coochie dancing, an early, supposedly sexually provocative belly dance from the late 1800s involving a short skirt with fronds hanging down.

Standing on the deck, I was always fascinated by the dance my father performed while setting the gear.

After he snapped the first leader onto the steel cable, he lowered the cannonball deeper into the water until there was enough space between the bottom line and the next one, and then snapped the next leader on. He repeated this until he had ten or twelve lines working in the water, snapped onto the four steel mainlines on the four gurdies.

Once he had all the leaders he wanted snapped onto the steel mainline, he swung the whole arrangement out from the side of the boat so that the lines were being tailed out from beneath the tops of the trolling poles.

But then the effect of the gentle swell rolling in from Queen Charlotte Strait started to make me feel queasy. Before I knew it,

I was throwing up over the side, hanging on to the steel guy wires that held the mast up. My dad was too busy to notice, deploying the gear on the other side of the boat. I felt a little better, breathing in deeply, inhaling the sea air. But that same fresh air blowing in from the northwest was cold, so feeling better now, while my father was busy setting the gear from the next set of gurdies and sending them drifting back on the pigs, I looked at the plywood skiff leaned up against the boom and realized I could squeeze myself in there, out of the wind. So I did.

Once tucked inside there, I felt snug and warm, kind of jammed in with my life jacket and very cozy. I could kind of peek out at the stern and watch my dad working the gear. After he got all four lines out, he looked up and made sure he was following the course he intended, putting slowly toward the northwest along the shore of Balaklava, heading toward Nigei Island to the west.

Once he had everything to his satisfaction, he looked up and then walked into the cabin. I thought he was just going to sit

My father, checking the tide book in the stern of his troller the *Seagull* in 1959. *Marcel Drouin photo*

inside, out of the wind, and steer from there for a while, but he was barely inside the cabin when he burst out again, running right by me looking all over, from side to side and then staring into the wake of the boat past the pigs. He was rushing back into the cabin when I stuck my head out from behind the seat of the rowboat and said, "Hi, Daddy!"

He turned red and exploded at me. It wasn't anything like I expected.

"I thought you'd fallen overboard!" he yelled. "I was looking all over for you. I thought you were in the bunk and when you weren't there and weren't on deck, I thought I'd lost you. You just about gave me a heart attack!"

After yelling at me, he went back into the stern to watch the poles for any action and to continue steering the boat along the shore toward Nigei Island.

Before long he started pulling gear. I was back out on deck now and watching what my dad was doing. The gurdies were powered by a complicated arrangement of belts and pulleys that started with a pulley mounted on the shaft behind the engine. Then there was a very long black rubber belt that ran up to a pulley on a brass shaft that went though the rear of the cabin and back to an old car transmission at the gurdies, where the transmission drove the gurdies on the port side of the boat. Another set of pulleys on the shaft was attached to another long rubber belt that ran through another pulley, and drove the gurdies on the starboard side of the boat.

To check the lines, he would shove a handle forward on whatever gurdy he wanted to activate and then it would engage and start turning, pulling the steel wire up. At intervals each leader would come to the surface, and if there was a fish on it, he'd pull it in, shake it loose into a holding box, and transfer the empty line over to the other side, where it would drag behind the boat while he pulled up the next one. Lines with no fish on them were just transferred over to the other side and hooked on a wire strung across the gunwale. If things were going well, he could transfer one empty line over to the other side while leaving the gurdy running and then scoot over to the side where the line was coming to the surface and stop it with the gurdy as it broke the surface. This had to be done swiftly to avoid the snap and leader going through the overhead pulley.

How he landed the salmon depended on what it was. Pink salmon, or "humpies" as we called them, had virtually no fight in them, so he could just pull the leader in until he got to the flasher, grab that, and swing the fish over the side and unhook it into the locker. Coho salmon had a lot more fight in them, so he usually used a gaff hook, leaning over the side and smoothly gaffing the fish in the head and swinging it aboard. Instead of the flashers and hoochies he fished on the top lines, on the bottom closest to the cannonball he usually had a big brass spoon called a Number Seven Wonder, which wobbled sideways like a herring. He hoped to catch the bigger chinook or spring salmon on those lines, and when he did, he had to use the gaff on them because they could get up to thirty pounds or even heavier, though they weren't real fighters like coho.

When he was finished pulling that set of lines, he did the whole process in reverse, setting the line with the brass spoon out first, then the lines with flashers on them, until they were all hooked on; then he retrieved the other lines, repeating the process all over again until all four cannonball mainlines had been pulled and reset. If he was trying for coho, he favoured green and white hoochies, and if he wanted pinks, he used pink hoochies, though pinks would bite coho gear. Cohos were worth a lot more, so he was fishing for coho most of the time unless there were so many pinks around that it was simply more lucrative to go for the volume.

I continued to watch with fascination as he worked the gear until all four lines had been brought in. When he had them all reset and fishing again, he changed course and came tacking back the same way we had come and started cleaning the salmon.

It was another complicated manoeuvre he had to do. In addition to steering the boat and watching all four mainlines that were trailing behind the boat, now he had to gut the fish. He had a specially built V-shaped trough that he put on the hatch cover in front of the little cockpit in the stern and put a fish in it. He swiftly removed the gills, throwing them overboard, then slit the belly from the anal vent to just behind the head, pulled the guts out, tossed them overboard; then, with a spoon affixed to the rear handle of his knife, he scraped the bloodline out from along the backbone. He tossed a bucket on a rope over the side, got a bucketful of water, washed the fish off, put it into the locker with ice in the bottom and repeated the process, all the while watching to make sure that everything was going okay.

Immediately he started tossing guts overboard, we were swamped by a flock of seagulls following the boat, diving down and gobbling up the guts as soon as they hit the water. Sometimes they would swoop out of the air and grab some right out of the air.

Other times, a gull would dive right underwater and go after them.

When my father pulled the guts out of the fish, most often the swim bladder would still be intact and the stomach and roe or milt sacs would be suspended in the water, held up by the air-filled swim bladder. A seagull would land on the water and peck at the guts underwater until it got a good portion in its beak and swallowed it whole.

I had a spare bucket on the boat, and sometimes I would retrieve a heart from my dad's flashing knife and drop it into the bucket of water. The disembodied heart kept working, sitting there throbbing in the bottom of the bucket as it pumped water now through its muscle.

Meanwhile my dad kept up his mechanical, methodical, steady cleaning of the fish—slice-throw, slice, pull, throw, scrape-wash and over again. I didn't know how to tell the different species of salmon apart then, even though I knew the huge ones were spring salmon, so I was asking questions while my father worked at cleaning the fish.

"What kind of fish is that, Daddy?" I asked. "How much a pound are we going to get for that one, Daddy?" I asked, as he continued.

"What did you do that for, Daddy?'

"What?" He stopped and looked up from under his waxed-canvas "Bone Dry" hat he always wore.

"You just kept the guts and threw the fish overboard."

He looked down at the fish cleaning trough and, sure enough, the guts were still there and the fish he had been cleaning was gone, sinking to the bottom.

"Why don't you just stop asking me questions all the time and let me clean the fish?" he yelled, raising his voice to me, something he rarely did.

We went back to Christie Passage to sell fish at Pete McWilliam's buying station, seeing as we had got ice there.

My dad was a pretty basic cook, particularly since all he had on board to cook with was a white-gas-powered Coleman camp stove. What I remember most about meals we ate on the boat is loaves of white bread, margarine and canned corned beef. My dad would rush into the boat while the gear was deployed out the stern, drop down into the tiny space beside the banging Easthope engine and quickly slap himself up a margarine, corned beef and mustard sandwich, and rush back outside before the boat veered off in some undesirable direction. I was left on my own to do the same or make a peanut butter and strawberry jam sandwich.

We didn't eat much fish on board, but one time I remember he boiled up potatoes in sea water and added a small jack spring cut up into thick chunks, then boiled everything until the fish was cooked through. It sure was salty.

At home he and my mother made perked coffee in an aluminum coffee pot with a little glass bubble on the top so you could see the coffee perking in it once it got boiling on the stove. I remember the odour of fresh coffee permeating the house before I got up, as my dad made a pot for his Thermos to take to work.

On the boat he brought a jar of Nescafé. As a child I never liked coffee when I tried it at home, and when I tried Nescafé I liked it even less, but on the boat my father brought it along for convenience. It was easy to boil water on the Coleman stove for his morning cup of coffee. The only time I ever saw sugar cubes was on the boat too. We never had them at home, but he bought some for the boat, again because they were so easy to use. If he didn't use them up over the summer salmon fishing season, though, and he forgot them on the boat, by next spring or winter-weekend fishing trip, they had absorbed so much moisture in the damp galley that they would dissolve into a soggy mess in the box.

We always had a can of evaporated milk on board, for his coffee and my cocoa, which I preferred to coffee, and I wasn't really a tea drinker as a child either.

He told me a canned milk story one time. He used to buy groceries for an old man who lived in a ramshackle house right at the edge of the water a short way down Stagger Alley, which is what everyone called the street that ran straight down the hill from the only corner in town, next to the big Burroughs house and the two-storey building on the corner. It's actually called Market Street.

Old Man Roy, as everyone called him, claimed to have been a member of Soapy Smith's gang in in Skagway, Alaska, at the time of the Klondike gold rush, fleecing gold seekers as soon as they got off the boat and ruining many before they ever left town. Anyway, he was illiterate and in his declining years somehow my dad did some shopping for him.

One day, after my dad delivered his grocery order, which included canned milk, Old Man Roy emptied out the paper bag onto the table and then asked my dad, "Where's the canned milk?"

"Oh, it's that can there," my dad said, pointing to a can of Carnation evaporated milk. The store had been unable to procure

Pacific-brand milk for some reason that week.

"That can't be milk," Old Man Roy said. "It's got a picture of a flower on it. Canned milk has a cow on it."

My father had a heck of a time convincing the old man that indeed it was canned milk, even if it didn't have a picture of a cow on it like Pacific did.

I went out fishing numerous times with my father in the summer, as they often had fire season shutdowns in the logging industry, so he got time off. Sometimes he even specifically took time off to go fishing, but not often. I didn't go in 1962 because that was the year my mom packed us kids up and we went to Quebec for the summer, a trip that had been aborted in 1960 when my sister got struck by a truck in Burnaby. My dad even took a few weeks off to come to Quebec to visit for the first time since 1952.

But there are many scenes from my last trip with my dad on the *Seagull* in 1964 that I still recall very clearly.

I remember going back to the Christie Passage fish camp in 1964, where again we took ice and sold fish. I had a camera with me that trip and only a few photos remain, but I still have a photo of some domestic grey geese that Pete kept, swimming round the dock. I also clearly remember going up to the store, the peculiar smell of the place from tar and fishing gear and the weird chocolate bar my dad let me buy. Most of the stock was sold out, so my chocolate bar was an unusual brand and strongly rum-flavoured.

We also moved along and fished out of a fish camp that was moored in a little cove on Hope Island in Bates Pass. Right adjacent to the floating fish-buying camp was an abandoned First Nations village, with some old, large two-storey houses still standing. I would have dearly loved to go ashore there, but when you are commercial fishing, if you are serious about it, you never go ashore.

Bates Pass leads out to Queen Charlotte Strait, where my dad wanted to fish. It's commonly called Roller Bay even though it isn't a bay at all, but that's fishermen for you.

Before I even woke up, my dad would start up the Easthope engine, untie the lines and putt out of the protected little harbour into Bates Pass. He would go out north through Shadwell Passage, past Vansittart Island on the right, and before we even cleared the island, he'd start setting the gear so that by the time we got out past the last point of land on Hope Island to our left, all the gear was out. Then he'd swing to the right and tack along, going east past the entrance to Shadwell Passage, outside the Nicholas Islands and toward Cascade Harbour and Cholberg Point. At Cholberg Point he'd swing to the southeast and follow the shore of Nigei Island all the way to Browning Pass. If fishing had been good, he'd turn around and follow the same tack back. If not, he'd swing northwest and head toward Pine Island in the middle of Queen Charlotte Strait, go almost right up to the lighthouse on the island, and turn back toward Hope Island, where we had started. Putting along at trolling speed, the round trip might take most of the day. If fishing was good along Nigei Island, he'd tack back and forth there all day, catching pinks and coho on the top lines and big spring salmon or ling cod on the bottom spoon.

When he brought in a ling cod in, it looked like he was pulling in a bucket of water full of teeth.

It was while we were trolling out in Roller Bay that we saw the troller *More Kelp*. It was a larger vessel than the *Seagull*, but without the elegant lines the *Seagull* had. It was boxy-looking.

"Why is that boat called the *More Kelp*, Daddy?" I asked.

My dad explained that the owner had previously owned a boat called the *Kelp*, so that when he built a new boat, he simply called it *More Kelp*.

The owner of the *More Kelp* was a man called John Daly from Garden Bay on the Sunshine Coast, near Pender Harbour. Later in life, he met New York writer Edith Iglauer and took her out on his boat as research for a book she was writing. They ended up falling in love and marrying, and *Fishing With John*, one of the best books ever written about trolling for salmon and the coast, was the result of that union.

We used to frequently see dolphins in the water. We didn't know that they were dolphins, so we called them porpoises. They didn't come around when we were trolling, because the boat went so slow, I suppose. But when we were travelling, even though the old *Seagull* probably didn't do more than six knots with a tailwind, they loved to come and play around the bow of the boat, scooting back and forth, exposing their backs and dorsal fins as they surfaced, dived and resurfaced again.

We did not see any live whales. They had started to get quite rare, seeing as commercial whaling was still occurring on the BC coast. But on a long straight stretch of shoreline on the northeast side of Nigei Island, a huge whale was beached above the high tide line. How it got washed up there and remained there, I don't know. It must have been washed up by a big storm with accompanying huge waves in combination with an extraordinarily high tide.

The stench of rotting flesh was overpowering even a third of a mile offshore. The seagulls, eagles and crows didn't mind, though. In fact, it was a bird magnet; the surface of the whale was virtually obscured by the flock of birds on the carcass, picking away, trying to open a spot on the hide to get at the flesh. I've often wondered over the past sixty-odd years if there is a bone left on that beach.

We would occasionally see orcas out in Queen Charlotte Strait.

The first time I saw them I was fascinated—the way they appeared out of nowhere in a group, coming to the surface and finning or coming partially out of the water, exposing their black bodies with white sides, with smaller ones sticking close to the medium-sized ones with medium-height fins, and usually one extra-large one with a high, prominent dorsal fin sticking out of the water much higher than all the others.

I suppose it is true that when the orcas come around, salmon will disperse—that was pretty obvious years later when I worked on salmon seiners in Johnstone Strait. But out there in Queen Charlotte Strait, the orcas were in transit from one place to the next or following a large school of salmon and didn't hang around. No matter—my dad had bought into the "they are our enemies" school of thought, and one day when we were trolling out near Pine Island, a pod of orcas started coming toward us. As they approached off to our port side, my dad ran into the cabin and came out with his .303 Lee-Enfield rifle and loaded it with cartridges as big as a man's middle finger.

The *Seagull* was putting along on course on its own, without anyone steering it, as the pod of orcas appeared alongside, travelling in the same direction as us about 150 yards away. My dad rested the stock of the rifle in his left hand on the edge of the boat and squatted down in the rear cockpit, sighting down the barrel of the rifle as the pod came broadside to us. There were several small whales that surfaced, exposing their flanks to us, then dived, too quick to shoot. The big bull appeared, a much bigger target and slower too, and when he was the most exposed out of the water with his black and white flank facing us, suddenly—*boom*—the rifle went off and a second or two later I heard *whoomp* as the 180-grain lead-tipped bullet struck the animal's side. The bull orca dove at the same moment and the entire pod disappeared underwater, never to be seen again. I have no idea how thick the flanks of an orca are, but I have seen the effects of those bullets on deer, bear, elk and moose, and they are devastating. The lead-tipped hunting bullet expands on impact, mushrooming and making a thick lead plug that penetrates deeply, damaging enormous amounts of tissue on the way. On an animal the size of an orca, though, the terminal energy of the bullet would probably be nearly exhausted before it even penetrated the animal's body cavity. If it did, what damage it could do to the lungs I don't know. Even if the bullet expanded and didn't penetrate the blubber, it would have made a hell of a painful wound that took a long time to heal.

***

Pine Island, in the middle of Queen Charlotte Strait, sat out there alone mostly shrouded in fog, the mournful sound of its foghorn blaring out through the mist.

I didn't realize it at the time, but Vivian Hunt, the little old Indigenous man whom I used to see occasionally around Port Hardy, had grown up at the Scarlett Point lighthouse on Balaklava Island, at the entrance to Christie Passage. Of Kwakiutl, Scottish and Tlingit heritage, he was among the middle of ten children born at the lighthouse. As soon as he was old enough, he delivered supplies and mail by rowboat from Port Hardy to Scarlett Point and to Pine Island. He still had a home in a little cove on Balaklava Island, tucked in behind the lighthouse. Even as an old man he used to regularly row into Port Hardy to buy essentials.

I remember one time when I was working on the log boom with my father in Port Hardy and we kept the boom boat down at Fisherman's Wharf. It snowed one night and there was six inches of snow on the ground. It was going to be tricky working on the logs with that much snow on them, but the trucks were still hauling logs out of the woods, so we had to go to work, of course. As we were walking along the snow-covered float to get to our dozer boat, there on the other side of the float, moored against it, was Vivian's rowboat. It had an oar propped lengthwise across the middle of it from bow to stern covered with a tarpaulin with a thick layer of snow on top of it.

The rowboat had not been there when we finished work and tied up the day before, so Vivian must have arrived in the evening, or possibly even in the night, though he was not known to travel on the water at night.

"Hey Vivian, are you in there?" I yelled above the snow-covered canvas. There was a long silence, and I was starting to fear that we were going to have to peel the canvas back to find his frozen body.

"Oh, yes, everything's fine," came his disembodied voice from under the tarp. He had simply put the tarp up over an oar when he had arrived and gone to sleep in there. He continued to commute from his home at Balaklava Island into his very senior years, but one day vandals burned his house down and, homeless, he ended his years by staying with friends in Port Hardy.

***

Sometimes my father would catch halibut on the bottom spoon if he ended up trolling close to the bottom. Sometimes he caught the bottom. Now, that wasn't fun.

I remember being aboard one time when he caught the bottom. It may only have been one cannonball, but it got caught in a crack in the rocks on the bottom, and all hell broke loose. The trolling poles bent over, and of course if he hadn't killed the engine, they could have bent backwards and broken, so he killed the engine. But once the engine was shut down, everything came to a standstill and every steel line that had been out with ten lines snapped to. The boat went dead in the water, so all the leader lines hanging down would potentially tangle with each other, and if we were that close to the bottom, then the bottom hooks were dragging in the seaweed and snagging there.

If a cannonball snagged on the bottom, my dad had to use the power gurdy at first to gently pull on it to try to get it loose, then to slack it off and pull it up again. In cases like that, if pulling gently didn't work he tried jerking it until the cannonball either came loose or ripped off the end of the steel cable.

I remember one time my dad spent hours retrieving each tangled line and untangling the snarl of wire and nylon leader, flashers and hoochies before he could get fishing again.

But when he got some halibut—boy, that was an event! For one thing, it was a challenge for my dad to even bring it over the side and into the boat. I don't remember my dad catching any "barn-door" halibut when I was with him, but even a thirty- to forty-pound halibut is quite a chore for a man who only weighs 128 pounds.

He knew he had something significant on the line just by the way the bell on the trolling pole was ringing, and he could tell by the way that the steel cable was pulled back that something big was on there. Then, when he got the cannonball to the surface, we could look back behind the boat and see what looked like a big dark-green blanket being pulled through the water.

He would have to pull that line in by hand and, when he got the fish alongside, somehow grab his gaff hook with a free hand and lean far enough over the side to gaff and swing it aboard in one movement, because if he had not done so, the fish would have started to fight to the end of the gaff hook and shaken it right out of his hands.

So, with one swift move, my dad leaned over, stuck the hook of the gaff under the fish's head and, carrying through, using two hands now, swung the whole fish up and over the side, into the fish-catching box in front of the cockpit. Even in the stiff westerly breeze the musky fragrance of the halibut filled the air as it lay there in the box, flapping so heavily that I could feel the vibrations several feet away on deck.

The hook came loose while the halibut flapped away in the box and my dad hit the fish on top of the head just behind the two eyes several times with the back of the gaff hook to subdue it, then left it to turn back to resetting the gear.

After pulling all the gear again, my dad had to get to the routine of cleaning the fish while he trolled for more fish. When he had finished all the salmon and tossed them down on ice, he went at the halibut. I had never seen one before. I had seen flounders before, and sole on occasion while fishing off the dock in Port Hardy or from my dad's little rowboat, which I took out frequently. But a large halibut was different. The grey-green mottled surface and the two prominent eyes on one side of the head, staring up at me, were striking. Now that it had been out of the water for a while, the pungent odour had passed. It wasn't the smell of rotten fish, far from it; it was an almost skunky scent.

My dad reached for the fish to start cleaning it, but it started flapping again at his touch, so he had to wallop it on the head yet again before he started the task of first removing the gills, which was a lot harder than cleaning a salmon because, unlike a salmon that lay neatly in the fish cleaning trough, the halibut of course lay completely flat. But he managed to get the gills out. Then, reaching down with his fish knife, he found the anal vent and sliced up the belly toward the head, making an opening large enough to get this hand in and extract the guts.

The summer of 1964 was the last one my father fished commercially.

He sold the boat to three guys who worked for the telephone company who wanted to use it for sport fishing. They didn't pay attention to it, though, and as it was an old wooden boat that leaked, it needed pumping out nearly every day. They didn't do that, and it sank at the float before the next summer.

It got pulled up on the beach by Fisherman's Wharf, and it wasn't long before it started to fall apart, with the tide coming in and out over it two times a day and the occasional log drifting in and bumping against it. I used to look at the poor old boat almost every day from about the autumn of 1965, when I was delivering the *Vancouver Sun*. I'd go down to the wharf too, to try to sell off extra newspapers that the *Sun* had sent me. The first thing that came off was the cabin and trunk cabin; then the planks and deck came off, and in two years the only thing left was the venerable Easthope engine. I wouldn't have been surprised if some of the parts of that engine were still useable. There were a lot of brass fittings on an Easthope. I read a story by Howard White in *Raincoast Chronicles* about salvaging Easthope parts off the beach on Minstrel Island to get his own engine going again.

10 / **Kickapoo Juice**

WE HAD BEEN FISHING on the *Seagull* out of Bates Pass for a week when early one afternoon at the end of a tack along the shore of Nigei Island my father said, "Let's go see if Shorty is home."

Shorty Sagar was a buddy of his from Port Hardy, originally from England, whose real name was Reginald. He had an alcohol problem and never had a regular job but was always engaged as a bull cook or a camp watchman.

That's what he was doing now. The Maloney brothers had a small logging claim on the northeast side of Nigei Island and the floating camp was shut down for the summer. Shorty was there making sure that everything remained intact and unvandalized.

This was the summer of 1964, when I was eleven years old. My father was thirty-nine at the time.

As we approached the entrance to Clam Cove, my father pulled all the gear, shaking what fish he had caught into the hold.

To get into Clam Cove was a bit of a challenge. Its entrance is very narrow and tucked between some small islands, so unless you know exactly where it is, you can go right by. But my father knew where it was and delicately guided the old *Seagull* through the narrow passage, the echo of the one-cylinder Easthope echoing back at us as we went through. The air was thick with the scent of the trees, a change from the wind and salty air aboard the *Seagull* out in Roller Bay.

Once through the narrow entrance, we came into this totally calm lagoon with the float camp nestled in it: a hodgepodge of buildings that included a floating workshop, a cookhouse, bunkhouses, a powerhouse and an outhouse perched over the water.

Some of the floats looked substantial, but some of the others looked half-sunk and I doubt if they were ever towed out to sea again.

Shorty emerged as we were tying up. He really was short, barely over five feet tall, and round in the belly and bald on top. He still had a residual English accent.

"Well, by Jesus, Jules, I didn't expect to see you today," he greeted my father as he tied up the bowline of the boat. "I didn't know you were fishing out here. How's the fishing been?"

My father told him about the fishing, the nice springs we were catching on the bottom lines and the coho and pinks on the upper lines. I don't think we were fishing pinks at that time with pink hoochies on flashers, but mostly coho with green and white hoochies behind Abe and Al flashers.

"Not bad," my father said. "I saved you a spring salmon if you want."

They got to talking and Shorty mentioned that he hadn't had a feed of fresh meat in a long time, and they decided that my dad was going to go into the hills of Nigei Island, on the logging road up behind camp, and shoot a deer.

So off we went with my dad's Lee-Enfield.

I think the camp hadn't been in operation for quite a while, because there wasn't a vehicle in sight, and not only was the road smooth and undisturbed by tires, but there were small trees starting to grow on it.

My dad loaded his rifle with a *ka-chunk*, put the safety on and started walking up the hill, with me tagging along behind.

Down close to camp the road went through a small stand of trees, and then the forest cleared away to small clear-cuts on both sides of the road where they had taken the logs from. It was in one of these that we hoped to see a deer.

It was starting to get warm already; it was August after all, and certainly not hunting season. Even I knew that.

We hadn't walked very far when suddenly my dad said, "There's one, don't move," and he raised the rifle. I tried to look in the direction the gun was pointed but couldn't see anything. Then the rifle went off. *Bang!* I was shocked at how loud it was. It hurt and my ears rang.

My dad lowered the rifle.

"I got it. Let's go," he said, and we started uphill through the tangle of brush, slash and small trees. I fell and skinned my shin.

We finally scrambled through the tanglefoot bush and got up to the deer. It was a doe. I think that even at eleven I realized that shooting a doe was illegal, even in season. The legs kicked out once or twice, then it was completely still.

I can't remember if I was horrified or what. It just seemed natural, I guess. We'd been killing fish all summer, after all.

My father laid his rifle down and manoeuvred the deer around so that he could work on it. He laid it out evenly in a spot as flat as he could find, then lifted the back leg so that the belly of the deer was exposed.

"Here, hold this," he said, handing me the hoof of the hind leg, then kneeled at the rear end of the deer and started dressing it out.

When he was done, he separated the liver from the rest of the guts, turned the deer onto its belly to drain most of the blood out, then wiped his hands off on some moss and pulled out his cigarettes. He smoked Sportsman plain cigarettes, the ones with a picture of a fishing fly on one side of the package and a guy in a canoe fishing on the other.

After he finished his smoke, my dad put the liver into the body cavity of the deer, hoisted it up onto his shoulders, with the front legs over one side and the hind legs over the other, and stood.

"Take the gun," he said, and started down through the slash to the road. We walked back to the float camp that way, with me feeling big and important carrying the rifle.

When we got down to the camp, Shorty helped my dad hang the deer up by its hind legs in the tool shed. They cut slots in the patch of skin in the back legs where the tibia met the femur, put a piece of wood between the legs with the ends stuck into each slot, spreading the legs apart, and hoisted the deer up.

After my father peeled the hide off, I remarked that it looked a lot like a person.

Shorty fried up the liver for dinner. Even as a kid I enjoyed deer liver, so we all had a good feed of liver and onions, mashed potatoes and canned peas.

Then they got into Shorty's "Kickapoo joy juice."

Shorty enjoyed his drink, and my father was known to not turn down an offer as well, but they had no store-bought liquor.

Shorty, however, had come up with his own concoction he dubbed "Kickapoo joy juice" after the moonshine in a popular newspaper cartoon at the time called *Li'l Abner*.

But Short's joy juice was not distilled hillbilly moonshine, but more of a jailhouse brew in a fruit juice base.

He made it in a ten-gallon aluminum stock pot. What I remember most is the halves of grapefruit floating in it, along with a few pieces of potato and the contents of numerous cans of fruit cocktail; a blend of diced pears, peaches with a few chunks of maraschino cherry thrown in, apples and maybe a few oranges, all sitting in the liquid with the yeast still actively bubbling and farting away in it.

I'd never smelled anything like it. It was sort of like the smell of my mother's rising bread dough, but sweet and fruity at the same time. It was appealing and disgusting, sweet and sour at the same time.

Shorty dipped a saucepan into it and strained out a couple coffee cups of the stuff, and they started drinking.

I went and played in the shop. Logging camp shops had a smell all their own, from the tubs of cup grease and oil, oil-stained wood and tools, rust and mould. It was fascinating. I found some paint cans and there was one tin with a worn label on it saying it was Prussian blue. I pried it open, and it gave off this rich linseed-oil scent.

I didn't even ask, but I went and got my dad's gaff hook and found some brushes and stirred up the paint and painted the whole handle Prussian blue.

I think I might even have cleaned the paintbrush off, but when we got back to fishing, that blue paint hadn't dried at all and my dad got his hand all sticky and blue when he tried to gaff a fish, so he had to wrap my nice, newly painted handle with a rag.

The outhouse on the float camp fascinated me. It was just a plain, ordinary old outhouse, but it was suspended on a platform over the water, so when you looked down through the hole, instead of seeing the pile of putrid human waste and toilet paper that usually lived there, you saw an aquarium. You could see pile perch and the occasional other fish swimming by when you peered in the hole.

Back in the cookhouse they kept drinking Shorty's Kickapoo juice and talking louder and louder about people they knew back in Port Hardy, chain-smoking cigarettes at the same time until I got bored and went off to my bunk on the boat.

My dad was feeling sick the next morning and didn't get up too early. We eventually did, though, and went into the cookhouse to see Shorty. He made a big pot of coffee and must have made some cocoa or something for me and breakfast for all three of us.

I think my father still had a little bit of ice in the fish hold even though we had sold the fish from earlier in the week.

I remember that when we got home and he told my mother he had to go down to the boat after dark to bring the deer meat in, she got mad at him for shooting a deer out of season.

My dad sold the boat after the season was over and that part of my life ended, as we didn't even go fishing on weekends anymore, so I had to start finding more things to do on my own.

When we had been fishing on the *Seagull* I was always fascinated by the shoreline, with its craggy rocks, pocket beaches and piles of logs driven up by the wind and tides, but except for going to the fish-buying station in Christie Pass and the logging camp at Clam Cove, I never got to explore ashore.

I decided that one day I was going to investigate the stretch of shore between Port Hardy and Duval Point, which I had seen so much of from the boat, so I started making plans to do that.

11 / Cliffhanging

LOOKING DOWN FROM THE CLIFF FACE where I was clinging over the swirling water below, with the tide at its highest point now, I realized that if I fell in and drowned, my parents would never know what had happened to me. Looking ahead along the cliff, I could see no more handholds, and looking back to where I had come from, I couldn't even see the cracks in the rock that had led me here. I didn't know what to do and started tingling all over. Then I looked up.

Easter weekend the year I was thirteen, I had a raging toothache. Having trouble with your teeth in Port Hardy was a perpetual problem. There was no dentist there, so you had to make a major expedition to Vancouver or Victoria to see a dentist. The best thing you could do if you had an abscessed tooth or something was go to the doctor and hope to get a prescription for antibiotics. Dr. Pickup in Alert Bay did extractions if necessary, but that wasn't a regular part of his practice. He was unconventional, though, and did what had to be done.

I didn't have access to a dentist, but I had a little vial of clove oil that I put on my tooth and around the gum periodically to dull the pain.

I don't know what got into me, it might have been the pain I was in, but I just had to do something to distract myself, so I decided to take my Diana air rifle and go for a hike. In those days, there was really nowhere you could go for a walk in the forest in Port Hardy unless you wanted to drive nine miles up the Holberg road and go into the meadows there, so the alternative was to go up rivers, where you could walk on the gravelly riverbanks and clamber over log jams or along the shore. I elected that Easter weekend to hike along the shore to Duval Point. I couldn't actually go to Duval Point, because Duval Point is on an island at the entrance to Hardy Bay, so I thought I would walk along the shore toward the point and see if I could get to Duval Channel, the little passageway between Vancouver Island and tiny Duval Island.

Duval Point was my father's favourite spring salmon fishing spot. I remembered that when he had the troller *Seagull*, we used to fish almost right up to the rust-streaked cliffs there.

I packed up a few essentials that morning and set off. I had some matches, my trusty .177 Diana air rifle, my Bowie knife and a can of baked beans. I didn't even think of taking a water bottle or canteen of any kind. There was usually plenty of water to be had coming down from the hills in streams.

We lived between the Glen Lyon River bridge and the M&B log dump at the time, so first I had to walk to town, then through town and down the road to the Tsulquate Indian Reserve.

When I reached the Tsulquate River bridge to the reserve at the northwest edge of Port Hardy, I remembered the time only a few years earlier when we found out that it was reserve land.

I had walked over to town to play with some of my friends when I was nine or so years old in 1962, and we had waded across the river and were shoving our way through the salal brush in the logged-over area uphill from the river. When we came to a large stump that projected above the salal, we found a piece of paper stapled to it declaring that it was Indian reserve. We laughed. Indian reserve? Here? That wasn't very likely. All the Indigenous people we knew lived out at Fort Rupert.

As children we didn't know the machinations that were going on between the Indian agents in Victoria and Ottawa to force the First Nations people from Smith Inlet and Blunden Harbour on the mainland on the other side of Queen Charlotte Strait to move to Port Hardy.

When I was very young, we knew that there were Indigenous people who lived in Blunden Harbour and were very different from the First Nations people we knew around Port Hardy. The village was called Ba'as and people there called themselves the 'Nak'wax-da'xw.

They used to come over to Port Hardy to go shopping once in a while, and sometimes a whole family or other large group would show up at Fisherman's Wharf in a rickety old boat that made me wonder how they safely got across.

One time I saw someone who looked like a wild man to me. He had very long hair for the time (this was before we'd ever heard of some band called the Beatles), a wispy beard and hip waders. He looked like some kind of Indigenous pirate, and we were scared of him. That was about all we knew of Blunden Harbour.

We had never even heard of the village of Takush in Smith Inlet. It was the home of the Gwa'sala people, the most northern tribe of the Kwakwaka'wakw.

What we also didn't know was that numerous families were soon going to be unwillingly dumped on Fort Rupert Kwakiutl Band land and forced to lived in incomplete houses with no plumbing or running water.

All we knew is that the government built a bridge at the Tsul-quate River and started building houses and then suddenly, in the autumn of 1963, there was whole group of new people living there and a whole bunch of new kids in the school.

It didn't go well.

For years, to make administration of health care and education easier and cheaper, the federal government had been trying to get the villagers of Takush and Ba'as away from their isolated communities, where they continued to live their mostly traditional lifestyles along with commercial fishing.

Officials promised the residents of Takush and Ba'as new houses, access to medical care, employment opportunities, schooling for their children and moorage for their fishboats if they moved. In addition, the Department of Indian and Northern Affairs threatened to cut off support for housing, education and other services if they stayed in their villages.

Lured by the promises, the villagers agreed to move, but were shocked when they did.

Twelve families moved to the new location in the autumn of 1963 and found that there were only six incomplete houses there for them.

By December 1968 there were 220 people living in twenty-three houses with no indoor plumbing or hot water.

In an interview in the *North Island Gazette* published December 4, 1968, James Walkus said that when the people arrived at the new village, they found that things weren't the way they were supposed to be.

"We were told that every house would have full plumbing but when we got here, we found that they only had one cold water tap and no toilets. Right now there is five outhouses for 22 or 23 houses, and they are in such tough shape that most people won't use them. They use chamber pots and go out and dump them in the river when they are full.

"Another thing they told us was that there would be enough houses for everybody, and we've never had enough."

Walkus said the authorities burned the old Blunden Harbour village in two stages, first in 1964 and then in 1965.

"They started building Tsulquate in the spring of 1963," said

Walkus. "And we moved over in the fall. We couldn't get back in the winter because our boats were too small for the kind of water we had to cross. Next spring, we started fishing so we were too busy to go back until fall. That was when we found some of the houses burned. The next year they burned the rest.

"I only know of one couple who was told their house was going to be burned. And they asked the man from the agency to give them time to get their stuff out of the house. He went ahead and burned the houses anyway with all the stuff still in them."

In addition to personal belongings, traditional valuables and regalia were destroyed in the fires.

Former Indian agent Alan Fry based his 1970 novel *How a People Die*, set in the fictional village of Kwasi, on the conditions in Tsulquate.

Of course, I never knew any of this background when I crossed the Tsulquate River bridge. All I knew was that most of the kids from the reserve that came to Robert Scott School had a hard time of it, being made fun of and openly discriminated against by the white kids and the Indigenous kids from Fort Rupert too. They spoke English with thick accents and dressed in poor clothing, and many were too shy to really interact with anybody. When I think about it now, they were probably frightened too and probably got attacked by the white kids on their long walk from the Tsulquate Reserve up to Robert Scott School.

***

One of the most embarrassing things that teachers can do to adolescent students is to try to teach them ballroom dancing. Now that I think about it, it was probably just as embarrassing for the teachers. But in the end, we all had to go through with it. Our homeroom teacher Mr. Madsen was this tall, gangly, dead-serious Dane and the woman teacher who helped teach the dance class was Mrs. Turnbull, this plain-looking woman with enormous breasts she attempted to control in those corset-like armoured bras of the day that made them look like the torpedo-shaped tail lights of a 1959 Cadillac.

They explained how the steps to a waltz were supposed to go, put on some music and demonstrated. In fact, they were good at it and glided around the floor as if they had done it all their lives.

And now it was our turn. Of course, the most painful part of the whole procedure was figuring out who was going to dance with whom. Naturally, the boys who were sports stars immediately paired up with the prettiest white girls, then the average-looking guys with average-looking girls, and then, when it came down to the very last pick, there was nobody left but Nadine from Tsulquate and me.

We were both mortified. I was scared and embarrassed and I'm sure Nadine was too.

I had nothing against Nadine; indeed, unlike many of my friends, I had nothing against anyone from Tsulquate, but I knew the way the bullies were going to react and tease me mercilessly if I danced with her. I was glowing red with embarrassment and could feel my ears burning when Mr. Madsen said, "Meeshul," (he never pronounced Michel correctly) "you will dance with Nadine."

So we met awkwardly on the floor and faced each other, and when the teachers had satisfactorily paired everyone, they instructed us in how to hold each other with one arm around the waist and the other holding a hand, and then they started the music again.

I had never held a girl close to me before and Nadine's hand felt damp and cold to mine, and I could feel the muscles of her back through her thin dress. We tried to match the one-two-three steps that the teachers had demonstrated but ended up stepping on each other's toes more than anything else.

There is a class photo around somewhere with Nadine in it, smiling broadly, but I don't think I ever saw her smile much in real life. I don't think the white girls were very kind to her.

Around this time I saw a television show called *The Education of Phyllistine*, based on a Paul St. Pierre story about the Chilcotin.

In the story, a First Nations girl is compelled to attend a non-Indigenous school to make up the ten students needed to qualify the school for a teacher. Maltreated by the teacher and other students, she stays for only one year. Some of the things I saw in that fifty-six-minute film could have been lifted right out of my classroom at Robert Scott School and the ways that the teachers and other students treated the kids from Tsulquate.

***

As soon as I crossed the bridge over the Tsulquate River, I walked down onto the beach and around the several beached, derelict fishing vessels there, then along the gravelly shore past the village, and set out on my beach walk. I had no idea that a year before, two young girls had died in a beached boat there when the tide came in while they were sleeping, taking refuge from an overcrowded house.

Beyond the Tsulquate village the beach was completely wild. When I say *beach*, I don't mean smooth, white, sandy beaches you see in holiday brochures; this was a rocky shore, and I was about to find out how rocky.

The shoreline between Tsulquate and Duval Channel was mostly outcroppings of rock between the water line and the trees at the edge of the forest. The tide was still partway out when I started, so I was able to walk along the bottom of the small cliffs of rock at first, but then, when the tide got a little bit higher, I had to start clambering across the rocks themselves. It wasn't long before I started regretting that I had brought my air rifle along. Some of the rocks I had to climb over were quite smooth, with very few cracks in them to provide either footing or handholds, so having to carry that stupid air rifle in my right hand meant I only had my left hand to grab for a crack in the rock or a small tree for safety. Plus, my tooth hurt. Climbing around on the bare rocks afforded no comfortable place to stop and rest, so I just kept going, climbing up the rocks above the water now, or right up to the edge of the trees, where there was sometimes kind of a path where the thick brush met the rocks. There was no question of going into the bush. It was so thick with salal, stunted trees and other brush that even a small dog would have had a hard time getting into it.

After clambering across a small rocky bluff, I descended into a bay with a broad, gravelly beach, a stream running down to the salt water and a pile of driftwood logs at the high tide line. I stopped there, had a drink and rested, dabbing my aching tooth with more clove oil before getting up and starting out again.

After an easy start, it was back to rock climbing again, skirting up above the water as the tide had really come in now, leaving no more opportunity to walk below the cliffs. As I continued along, I finally got some respite when the cliffs gave way to a low, rocky beach and then a small, but flat, gravelly shore before the rock bluffs climbed up to the trees again. After getting across the next series of cliffs, I found a low point below the rocks I could easily navigate, and got away from hanging over the water for a change.

But my relief was short-lived. Soon I was back to rock scrambling, regretting more and more that I had decided to bring my air rifle along. What was I going to do if I encountered a bear or a cougar anyway? Sting it and hope it would go away? Despite many people fearing bear and cougar encounters, I had never had any trouble with either; bears always took off running in the opposite direction if you came upon them and I had never seen a live cougar.

I spent the next hour scrambling over more rocky shore until I came to another beach. By now I was getting hungry, and besides, that tin of beans in my bag was bugging me, with its weight banging awkwardly against me as I tried to manoeuvre across the steep rocks. So I decided to stop and eat the beans.

I gathered up as many small pieces of wood as I could get, but finding dry wood even on a nice day around Port Hardy is not easy.

By going up to the edge of the high tide line and looking under the edges of big logs, though, I could at least find drier wood than what was lying around lower down on the beach.

I must have thought to bring paper along with me, because without a little bit of newspaper to burn it is damn near impossible to get a fire going on the coast. I broke up the smallest and driest little sticks and twigs I could find, split a piece of cedar up with my sheath knife, crushed up my paper, piled the smallest wood pieces on top of the paper and lit it. The paper flared up and the wood smoked, but as the paper continued to burn away, the wood just didn't catch. I squatted down in the gravel and blew and blew at the remains of paper, making it glow red as a few of the twigs half-heartedly tried to flame up, but eventually the whole thing just fizzled out into a barely smoking mess of unburned wood.

I dismantled the pile of wood, took one of the larger pieces and split it into kindling, found a few more dry, small pieces of wood and, using the last scrap of paper that I had brought along, tried again to light my fire. This time flames started licking up from the paper to the small pieces of wood as they caught fire; the next layer of wood caught, and despite producing a huge cloud of white smoke at the same time, the fire caught and soon I had a decent blaze going.

Once the first of the larger pieces of wood had burned down a bit, I dug my can of beans out of my shoulder bag, stuck it into the fire and piled up some more wood around it so that it would heat evenly.

I looked out to the little island just offshore from the nook in the rocky shore I was resting in and started idly wondering what it would be like on that island with its scraggly trees. Maybe I should come back with a rowboat one day and check it out. I watched the seagulls fly over and noticed a grebe or surf scoter between me and the island, periodically diving and sometimes coming up with a fish that it hungrily swallowed before diving again. Maybe

I should have brought a fishing rod instead of my air rifle. I might have been able to cast offshore and catch a rock cod or tommy cod or something to roast on the fire. Then I started thinking that I really should invest some of my paper route money in a spincast set. I'd always had only trolling rods and reels because I only fished for salmon while trolling out of a rowboat.

Then I looked into the fire, thinking maybe my beans were close to ready. I had been daydreaming too long. The other wood had caught fire and was busily burning away and there, in that mini-inferno, my can of beans was swelling up, looking more like a small barrel than a can now. I quickly kicked the fire apart and rolled the can out of the fire. Afraid still that it was going to burst like a grenade, I grabbed my big sheath knife and stabbed the tip of the blade into the top of the can.

Boiling-hot baked bean juice squirted out at me and got me on the hand holding the knife and across my cheek and forehead. I wiped it off my face and hand and then let the rest of the over-heated juice bubble out of the hole. I had to wait until the can cooled down before I could finally use my knife to cut open the rest of the lid and scoop out the beans with the spoon I'd brought. That's how I learned that you should pierce a can of beans before you put it in the fire, not after.

I had to eat the beans with only one side of my mouth, but even then the heat from them hurt my aching molar on the other side of my head. When I finished the beans, I dabbed another dose of clove oil on my tooth and gums.

After feeding on my beans, which had of course stuck to parts of the can in places where it had become too hot, I threw the can into the water to hopefully rust away and packed up for the rest of my trip. If I kept at it, I might be lucky enough to get to Duval Channel and turn around and be back before dark. My parents didn't know where I was, and I didn't want them to get worried.

Climbing the first rocky cliff after lunch was the start of a climb across the rocks above the water that lasted the rest of the morning. If I thought that I had covered some tough ground already, I was about to be surprised.

From my lunch point to Duval Island was punctuated by one rocky promontory after another. Some were nearly treeless, and I was simply able to walk across the bare rock. I even had a break with a couple of small, gravelly beaches I was able to walk on to easily make time.

I couldn't see ahead, of course, so I had no idea how much farther I had to go, but as long as it looked like I had time to keep going, it didn't cross my mind to turn back. I had a destination in mind. After a relatively easy passage across another beach, a rockpile I could easily climb over, and another short beach, the cliffs started to get steep, and I had to start finding footholds in the rock to steady myself.

I was on a peninsula now that jutted to the east out into Hardy Bay. It was fringed with trees right to the top of the cliff, so there was no opportunity to sneak along the edge of the trees above. I thought I had it made when, three-quarters of the way along the peninsula, there were no more trees, so I was able to easily walk across the top and west again toward the little cove at the end of the peninsula. From the highest and farthest point of the peninsula, I could see one more little point of land I had to get around and there was Duval Island, poking out into Goletas Channel.

Now on the north side of the peninsula, I looked toward the little cove I was aiming for to the west, and saw that the cliff facing me was virtually vertical. If I wanted to make it all the way to Duval Channel, I was going to have to make my way across that straight face or turn around and go home. There were even fewer foot- and handholds on this face than on any of the others I had encountered so far.

Gripping my rifle in my right hand and nudging my shoulder bag aside so it wouldn't get between me and the rock, I started edging my way across the sheer cliff.

But I couldn't find any more cracks in the rock to put my feet or hands in. And now I realized too that I shouldn't have started out with my rifle in my right hand. It was my leading hand and I needed that to reach out first and hold myself up as I inched across the rock. But now I couldn't go forward because I had run out of anything to hold or step onto.

I looked down at the eddying water below me as the tide had came in, something I shouldn't have done. I started tingling all over, right out to my fingertips and toes, and felt like I was going to tip over backwards even though I was stuck like a fly on that wall.

The water below me was obviously way over my head, and with the smooth rock face all along the shoreline below, there would be nothing substantial to grab hold of and pull myself out. I would drown for sure.

I had to decide. I couldn't stay clinging to that rock face all day. And now my toothache was throbbing away too, distracting me from trying to get out of this jam. Why had I brought this stupid air rifle with me? I should at least have improvised a sling so I could carry it on my back. I couldn't let go of the rifle or I'd lose it, and I couldn't transfer it to my left had because then I would not be hanging on to the rock wall at all. Looking up, I noticed that there were more fissures in the rock face than where I was stuck. Manoeuvring ever so slowly, slug-like even, I waggled my left hand up until I found a crack, testing it for security, then found a place for my right foot a little higher than my last foothold and pulled and pushed myself up. I lifted my left leg up to a crack too, and having gained a foot in elevation, rested a moment, my non-swollen cheek against the rock wall.

I had to get out of here. The tingling all over stopped. I kind of went into a zone I'd never entered before. A calmness came over me as everything else left my mind. I didn't even think of what was below me anymore. I didn't even feel my toothache anymore. I could see that if I could gain a few more feet up this rock face, it curved away at more of an angle toward the bush and trees at the top of the cliff.

I had both feet in a decent crack now, and looking up and to the right I could see another fissure I could get my hand in and a little shelf of rock I could lift my feet into, so I reached with my left hand, held on tight and then shifted my right foot up a notch and lifted myself up again one more level. I was now at a slight angle forward, with no more danger of slipping backwards, so I transferred the rifle to my left hand, leaving my stronger right hand and arm free to pull me farther up the rock. With another heave and pull I reached a portion of the cliff that sloped away more gently, and after a few more cautious motions to get there, I was finally able to get up on my feet and walk on the flattening surface at the top of the cliff where the trees shoved their way out of the forest.

I sat down, put down my gun, took off my shoulder bag and treated my aching tooth and gums with a dose of clove oil.

After the anesthetic took effect on my tooth, I looked around. There was a narrow little bay below me, and across from me another rocky shore like the one I had been traversing all morning, leading out to another peninsula similar to the one I had just come around. I could see Duval Island rising up just beyond that, and farther out past Duval Island, the Gordon Group of islands, with the largest, Doyle Island, towering above the rest.

After resting a bit, I realized I had better get going. I had no more food with me except a chocolate bar and I didn't want to go hungry. It was too early for berries, even though the salal bush grew thickly at the forest edge here.

Pretty soon I found myself out on the next peninsula over. I traversed that, and after another scramble across the rocks at the treed edge of the forest, I finally reached the rocky knob that stood at the entrance to Duval Channel. The water seemed deep right in front of me, but halfway across the channel a thick kelp bed filled the water all the way to Duval Island.

Sitting there on the rock, I contemplated my morning so far and watched some sea ducks diving around the edges of the kelp bed opposite me. The fragrance of the kelp hit me too, blended with the salty air and fresh fragrance of cedar and spruce from the surrounding trees.

Looking over at Duval Island and its thickly wooded shore-line just over a hundred yards away, I recalled the times several years before that, in the early 1960s, when I was aboard my father's little commercial troller and we fished in the deep water close to Duval Island on the Goletas Channel side. When we were adjacent to islands, I always wondered what it would be like to go ashore there. I could see now that it was as thickly wooded as the stretch I had just spent the better part of the day traversing, if not thicker. There wouldn't be much to see there unless I was willing to really push into the bush and look for any paths at all through the thick coastal tangle. It sure didn't look that easy to penetrate on this side of Duval Channel.

I was getting hungry now and I regretted not packing more food.

Now I had to get back. A least now I knew what the toughest parts of the hike were and what to avoid on the way back. I was not going to subject myself to clinging hopelessly to sheer rock faces, unable to go forward or backward.

Before getting up for the hike back, I reflected on what I should have done. I should have left the air gun at home, that was certain. If I had known how hard climbing around on cliffs was going to be, I might have tried harder to climb along higher up where the cliffs met the trees. That was what I planned for the hike home.

Knowing the layout of the land better, I avoided the cliffs I had been nearly stuck on, and when I came to those spots, I stayed up at the tree level. Even if I had to grab branches and small trees to get over some of the steep places where there was little or no footing, at least I had something to hold on to above me. As long as they didn't pull out. Fortunately, they didn't. Walking along the gravelly shore of some of the beaches I came to, I noticed that the tide was starting to recede, so in some places, rather than having to hang from branches above or scale sheer cliffs to make my way, I would be able to walk along the exposed shore at the bottom of the cliffs.

I couldn't do that yet, though, so I was soon back on the rocks, scrambling along while carrying the rifle in one hand and holding on with the other when I had to. But the hard part was over. I knew where I had to avoid the sheer rock cliffs and went above them.

Finally, as I got closer and closer to the reserve at Tsulquate, the tide went out far enough that I was now finally able to walk. Soon I reached the reserve itself and crossed the bridge over the Tsulquate River. After a short walk through town, past Fisherman's Wharf and across the Glen Lyon River, I was back home, just before dark.

The fragrance of a shepherd's pie was wafting through the house as I walked in the door.

"Where were you? I could have used a hand cutting wood," my dad said.

12 / **1965**

My FATHER SOLD the *Seagull* in the spring of 1965, so as summer approached, I didn't have commercial fishing to look forward to anymore. But a lot of other opportunities for adventure arose.

Whenever I start telling a story that starts with "I remember in 1965..." my sister gives me heck, saying, "Why do you say everything happened in 1965?"

Well, it's because I have some very vivid memories of that year, particularly the summer.

That was the year I went on a boat trip and did some log booming with Einar Johnson, that I spent two weeks with my dad up at the logging camp at the Nahwitti River, and also, at the end of the summer, when we took the bus down-Island and all the way to Vancouver and stayed with the Flanagans in White Rock. So yes, a lot of things happened in 1965.

In 1964 I had spent most of the summer on the *Seagull*. At eleven I could already run the gurdies on one side and even had a notion that in a year or two I could take the boat out myself, as soon a I was strong enough to turn the flywheel myself to start it.

Shortly after school got out in 1965, when I was twelve, I was hanging around down at Fisherman's Wharf as usual and made my way onto Einar Johnson's old boat, the *Canadac*.

Einar was a local, and he loved kids and I was one of them.

The boat had been involved in the pilchard and salmon fisheries in the 1930s, powered by a huge old three-cylinder Atlas engine with a flywheel almost as tall as me.

Einar lived on the boat when he wasn't off up the coast logging somewhere. He always seemed to enjoy having kids around, and unlike today, our parents had no worries that he was some kind of perv or pedophile, and some of us got to spend weekends or even longer on boat trips with him.

Einar seemed to alternate between being on a very strict health kick and going on a roaring drunk. When he was drunk, we didn't like hanging around on his boat with him. He introduced our family to wheat germ. He swore it was the cure to all our ills. He always had some carob beans around and encouraged us kids to chew on them instead of chocolate bars.

There were many stories about Einar circulating around Port Hardy when we were kids. How many were true and how many were fiction we'll never know, but they were all good stories.

One story claimed that he had stolen a boom of logs from another logging tow by pulling up at the back of the tow at night, moving the kerosene lanterns on the back corners up to the corners of the next boom, where the rear boom was attached to the others, and disconnecting it.

I know for sure that when my friend Kevin went to Bull Harbour with Einar, they "salvaged" gensets and other equipment from the coast guard station there by pulling them onto a float using the *Canadac*. While other loggers on the islands were short of equipment, he was also rumoured to have "lost" everything from sledgehammers to a Caterpillar tractor when he was cost-plus logging for the war effort.

His mulligans were the stuff of legend as well. He was famous for starting a stew of potatoes and rockfish for example, maybe throwing in a duck when that got depleted and adding whatever else became available. My friend Clifford said that the first time he ate bear meat was on the *Canadac*.

Einar liked to pull somebody's leg once in a while. There is one tale that Einar and his friend Bob Murray were in the snake pit in the Alert Bay hospital, drying out from delirium tremens, and Einar said to Bob, "Hey Bob, did you know Mike LeCerf and Skookum Charlie were out on the beach digging clams with your new McCulloch chainsaw?"

Einar was based on Quadra Island in the 1930s. He bought the *Canadac*, built on the standard forty-eight-foot seine boat pattern of the day, in 1935. It had been a pilchard tender before that.

Einar and his brother and father used the *Canadac* as a camp tender up in Bute Inlet in the winter, and then in summer, his oldest son Harold recalled, they painted her up for salmon season.

Einar didn't skipper the *Canadac* for seining, but hired captains to do that. In 1938 he bought a second seine boat, the *Cape Sun 32*. In an article about Einar in the magazine *West Coast Fisherman*, Harold said that the *Canadac* was high boat on sockeye for the whole West Coast fleet.

In 1939 Einar moved his floating logging operations to Knight Inlet. When war broke out, his company was conscripted to go to the Queen Charlotte Islands to log airplane spruce for the wood-framed Mosquito bombers.

After the war, Einar and Harold stored their logging camp in Port Hardy and went to Vancouver, where they owned Kanata Marine Ways until 1947.

When he retired the *Canadac*, Einar bought an ex–lobster boat from the East Coast, named it the *Sea Logger* and, in addition to towing logs with it, converted it to gillnetting, fishing for Seafood Products in Port Hardy.

Einar like to take kids out on his boat too. He'd been close to Harold and had worked together from the time when Harold was very young, and I think Einar missed that. Harold said that he had been running a camp and crew boat at the age of twelve.

One of my oldest friends from Port Hardy went out with Einar the week that the big earthquake hit Alaska on March 27, 1964. They had dropped in on Shorty Sagar, who had been watching the floating logging camp in Clam Cove on Nigei Island when the earthquake hit. In the morning most of the float camp was shoved much higher up onto the shore than it had ever been on a high tide.

After that, they went to Bull Harbour on Hope Island, on the edge of Queen Charlotte Strait opposite Vancouver Island. Once you leave Bull Harbour, you are facing the North Pacific Ocean. When they got to Bull Harbour, my friend was so terrified of another earthquake and tidal wave that he had a complete breakdown and begged Einar to get him out of there, and so Einar called a seaplane from Port Hardy and the local bush pilot Dave Stronach flew him home COD.

The week I went with him, Einar was planning to move the boat across the bay to boom up some logs that he had, and then to take a trip up Goletas Channel to the islands of the Gordon Group. Ever the audacious kid who wasn't used to hearing the word "No," I talked him into taking me along.

So, the morning that we were to head off, he showed me the accommodations down below. You had to climb down a narrow ladder that had metal edges into the engine room that housed the big three-cylinder Atlas. The engine room smelled of oil and grease and the rotten-egg stink of old bilge water. He showed me the bunk I could sleep in and warned me, "Don't you go and piss in the flywheel pan like that Jackie Wright did." Jackie was an older boy who had also hung around with Einar when he was younger.

The only reference Einar made to anything adult was when he was drinking and he'd suddenly say, in a thick, fake French-Canadian accent, "I sucked on it once and *nevair* again!"

We didn't have a clue what he was talking about, but I think in retrospect that it had something to do with a French-speaking girlfriend of his from way back in the past. We always thought Einar was old, of course, though he was probably only in his fifties when we knew him.

Starting the old Atlas was like starting my dad's old one-cylinder Easthope engine, except that instead of a small flywheel about three feet across, this one on the Atlas was much bigger and heavier. Whereas my father was able to hand-start the Easthope by cranking the flywheel around until the motor was under compression, then flipping it over past the compression point to make the motor fire the first time, Einar had to use a big iron bar to turn the flywheel on the Atlas.

When it started, though, it farted and burped and then started running very slowly with a deep-throated *ka-chuff ka-chuff*, as the flywheel kept turning around and around. To a twelve-year-old kid, this was fascinating.

Once we untied the lines, we didn't go very far. We just exited the inner harbour of Hardy Bay, cruised along the shore and pulled into Bear Cove.

Einar had a float with several buildings on it tied up there, and had a small booming ground. He was making up a log boom to be sold to a buyer down south.

To be honest, I can't remember where the logs came from. I know Einar wasn't doing logging anymore at all. He used to have small handlogging claims up and down the coast, but not anymore. These were probably salvage logs. In the mid-'60s it was still easy to get a log salvage licence to collect stray logs from booms found adrift and on the beach.

So Einar had a bunch of random logs collected in a log pen in the water and he wanted to put them together into a "section" for the towboat to pick up and tow to a mill ln Vancouver. A section was effectively a square sixty-six feet across. You had a "head stick" and a "tail stick," which were logs sixty-six feet long, and side sticks that were also sixty-six feet long.

Einar had caulk boots, but I didn't, so while he had the nails on the bottom of his soles to help him keep his footing, I only had running shoes. We were both out there on the logs, pushing them around, trying to get them into the correct slots between other logs, which is difficult, because if you are standing on one floating log and trying to pull or push another floating log along, the log you are on is just as likely to move as the one you want to move.

Eventually, the inevitable happened: I fell in. With no life jacket on, of course. Somehow, I managed to hang on to the side of a log long enough for Einar to come and pull me out. Now we had a problem. I was soaking wet and hadn't brought a change of clothes. So Einar outfitted me in the same garb that he was wearing: heavy wool tweed trousers and a grey Stanfield's wool pullover—only they were about six sizes too big, me being a skinny twelve-year-old.

Like I said, the wool tweed pants were heavy. They were the Pioneer-brand brown Bannockburn tweed sold by Jones Tent and Awning in Vancouver. Einar outfitted me with a set of suspenders too, and after we rolled them up to about half their length, I was able to get back out onto the logs until we finished making up the boom. And I didn't fall in again.

I wish I could remember what we ate. Einar ordered his "health foods" from either Famous Foods in Vancouver or another place.

After booming up the logs, we reboarded the *Canadac* and set off out of Hardy Bay into Goletas Channel and headed northwest, travelling with the Gordon Group of islands on our right and the thickly forested shore of Vancouver Island on our left. I was familiar with the sight, as that was the way my father had travelled with his small commercial troller.

As the old Atlas engine chuff-chuffed down in the engine room, Einar let me steer the *Canadac* with its great big old-fashioned spoked steering wheel. I had idly turned it around at the dock, but this was the first time I got to use it in action. It was hard to turn, with its strictly mechanical chain-and-sprocket mechanism turning the big old rudder in the stern, but fortunately, the *Canadac* made way in a straight line and all I was really doing was symbolically holding the wheel. The boat steered itself.

I had time to look around. Einar had 9mm pistol cartridges on the shelf in front of the wheel, holding the compass in its binnacle. Einar was rumoured to have a Luger pistol, but I never saw it. He had the ammo though. There were also several long, pencil-like cartridges for his 6.5x54mm Mannlicher-Schönauer carbine he had up over his bunk. I never saw Einar take that rifle down, but I sure admired it from a distance every time I went on the boat.

"What kind of gun is that, Einar?" I asked him one time. The stock of the rifle had been broken and a splint of thin wood had been attached with a course of green fishing twine wrapped around to repair it.

"Oh, that's a *Man-Licker*," he replied, and having seen full-stocked Lee-Enfield surplus military rifles in the Eaton's and Simpsons-Sears catalogues, I was convinced that it too was an "army gun," as I thought of them at the time.

I saw a box of ammunition for that rifle sitting out on top of a piling down at the Seafoods cannery a year later. It was just sitting there, fresh from the store at the time, I guess; someone must have dropped it while going down to the boat. It could have been Einar, for all I know, but nobody picked it up and it sat out there in the rain until the cardboard disintegrated and the cartridges spilled out of the box, and eventually they all rolled or were pushed into the water.

The air inside the small cabin of the *Canadac* was rich with the combined odours of the oil cook stove, the hot engine stench coming up from the hatch to the engine room, Einar's rarely (as in never) washed bedding, his clothes and drying fish hanging from the ceiling.

After several hours, we came to Christie Passage, between Hurst Island on the right and Balaklava Island on the left.

I remembered Christie Passage very well, as I had visited the little fish-buying station there on my father's little troller on numerous occasions. Pete McWilliam was still there, buying fish and selling basic supplies from his little store. There were huge fuel tanks there too, filled during regular trips by the Imperial Oil company's small fuel tanker. The 1962 painting *Christie Pass, Hurst Island* by E.J. Hughes shows the oil tanker tied to the dock there.

McWilliam had a small flock of domestic geese there too. I remembered that clearly, because I had taken photos of them.

We carried on until we got to the Scarlett Point lighthouse on the tip of Balaklava Island, where Queen Charlotte Strait opens and you can sail almost in a straight shot to Cape Caution on the other side, passing Pine Island on the way.

I had seen the Scarlett Point lighthouse many times already, since that was the route my father took to go fishing out in Roller Bay. I had been fascinated by the station, with its tall, white, red-topped light tower and neatly tended white buildings and red roofs.

The buildings and light tower were all built on a tiny peninsula of Balaklava Island, with the forest backing them and all the trees removed from the land in the front and sides to give maximum visibility to the light from the sea. Somehow, the keepers had even managed to coax a lawn out of the thin soil surrounding the buildings.

Einar stopped there and we went ashore. I remember how welcoming the lighthouse people were and how clean and neat and tidy the keeper's house was. Extremely tidy. Nothing out of place and licked completely clean. I think they offered Einar coffee or tea and they gave me a glass of Sun-Rype lime juice: from a tin, of course. Everything came from tins in those days.

Pretty soon we were on our way back to Port Hardy, and that was the end of my excellent adventure with Einar. But it wasn't long before I got another taste of booming logs—only the next time, it was with my dad.

13 / Nahwitti, 1965

DO YOU KNOW WHAT "Help!" sounds like when you are five feet tall and standing on the bottom of a river in six feet of water, anchored down by a pair of heavy logging boots?

I turned twelve in June 1965, and later in the summer I went up to the logging camp at the mouth of the Nahwitti River about thirty miles west of Port Hardy on northern Vancouver Island to stay with my father, who was working there for O'Connor Logging.

My dad was working on the boom up there, and before my mom was going to take us kids down to Vancouver to go to the PNE and see some friends in White Rock, I was allowed to go stay in camp and see what my dad did for a living.

When my dad came home on one of his rare days off, he agreed to take me with him. There was a bunk available in the bunkhouse he was in, so that was one of the reasons that I was allowed to go.

So, with several changes of clothes packed up by my mom for the trip, I joined my dad down at Fisherman's Wharf to board the boat the *Sea Logger* for the trip along the east coast of Vancouver Island to the mouth of the river where the camp was situated. I didn't realize it then, but it was near the site of a former First Nations village. I'm sure the mouth of the river was used for salmon fishing in season, though, even if the main village was closer to Cape Sutil, just a little bit farther up the island's coast to the northwest, toward Cape Scott.

The First Nations village at Cape Sutil was also the site of what came to be called the Nahwitti Incident, a battle between the Hudson's Bay Company, the British navy and the local First Nation, known today as the Tlatlasikwala, part of the larger Kwak-waka'wakw First Nation.

The Cape Sutil Nahwitti village was a major site for the fur trade between 1790 and 1850. The actual harbour used for trade was in nearby Shushartie Bay, south of the Nahwitti River.

There are several different versions of the story, but it appears that the whole thing was the result of a misunderstanding in 1850. Three indentured servants of the Hudson's Bay Company deserted in Victoria and accidentally boarded the barque *England*, headed north instead of south toward their intended destination of California. They disembarked at Fort Rupert and, after borrowing or stealing a canoe, paddled to Hope Island. The Hudson's Bay Company posted a reward for their return. It remains unclear what really happened, but the three were killed, and the HBC accused the Nahwitti people of murder, which the Nahwitti denied. In 1851 the Royal Navy was sent in with sixty men to apprehend three Nahwitti men accused of the murders, and after burning the unoccupied Nahwitti village on Nigei Island, the navy went to the Cape Sutil village. After a battle (in which the village was shelled, according to some reports), the three suspects in the murder and a chief were killed.

But that was all well over a hundred years in the past, and we didn't know anything about it at the time.

The *Sea Logger* was a former lobster boat that someone had imported from the East Coast on the railway and equipped with a tow bit. Besides being used to transport crew and groceries up to camp, it was the towboat that hauled away the log booms that my dad was constructing.

Peter Spencer, with his engineer's cap ever perched on the back of his head, ran the boat.

I had been part way up Goletas Channel with my father on the *Seagull* about a year before, but this time, instead of going through Christie Pass, we continued northwest along the eastern shore of Vancouver Island. The roar of the diesel engine powering the *Sea Logger* made it nearly impossible to talk, so I just looked out at the shoreline.

I always had my eye open for a bear beachcombing the shore but never saw one.

We motored past wide, deep Shushartie Bay before entering the mouth of the Nahwitti River and docking at the float in front of the camp.

O'Connor had a vibrant logging camp stretched out along the bank of the river, with a row of bunkhouses strung along to the right as you walked up the ramp toward the cookhouse and office building, and farther upstream, a shop and marshalling yard for the loggers.

I don't recall if they even had built a road decent enough for a vehicle to drive on, and I never really went farther up the river than the estuary, where they had a booming ground where my dad worked. So I assume that the loggers had to walk up the skid road to where they were logging.

They skidded the logs out of the woods with a thing called an "arch." The arch was just that: an arched, heavy steel A-frame mounted on big rubber wheels. It had a pulley up at the apex of the A and was attached to the rear end of a powerful Caterpillar tractor. A winch cable went up from the rear of the Cat, up through the pulley on the arch and down to the log that it was going to pull out of the woods. There was a choker system with multiple cables so that the Cat could pull several logs at once or one big one, depending on the size. The logging crew would choke the end of the logs, hook them up to the tow cable, and the Cat operator would lift the ends of the logs off the ground and then drag them down the skid road to the river flats in the estuary. When the camp was established by the Eilertsens, long before O'Connor Logging took it over, they excavated a pond in the estuary with their Cat to create some depth in the river mouth to make a booming ground.

You could never do that today because of regulations protecting fish habitat, but that wasn't even considered in the 1960s.

When the tide was out, the mud flats of the estuary dried up, so the Cat operator would drag the logs as far out into the mud as he dared without getting bogged down, release the logs, and go back for as many more "turns" as he could perform before the tide came in.

When the tide did come in, my father went to work. His job was to put the logs together in a floating raft called a boom. He had started his logging career as a pulp faller and river driver in Quebec and Ontario and had been working on the coast ever since.

They had a booming ground set up, with permanently anchored "stiff-legs": a rectangular frame of logs fixed in place in the deeper, wider part of the river where he could make up the log booms.

The loggers would select the nicest, straightest logs with as little taper as possible for "boom sticks," and the Cat operator would bring them down to the estuary and pile them separately for my dad to work on. They had to be exactly sixty-six feet long.

Using a four-inch auger connected to a chainsaw motor, he had to drill a hole through each end. This was so that they could be connected to each other with six-foot-long boom chains, to make a framework of logs around the logs that would get towed away to market.

How he was able to drill holes in those logs by himself, I have no idea. Maybe he got one of the chokermen to help him on the day he had to bore some sticks. Seeing as I was there with him, he got me to help. There were two sets of handles on the motor, much like bicycle handlebars. On my dad's side he had the controls, and on the other side, facing him, was the other set. The auger stuck out of the bottom of the machine.

He would start the motor with the pull cord, leave it in neutral, then indicate that he wanted to lift it up. Then he would position the end of the auger in the spot where he wanted to drill the hole through the log, engage the clutch and let the auger start to turn. At twelve, it was all I could do to hold on to the other side. Once the motor was engaged, the auger would chew into the wood and start drilling.

Periodically, he would look at me and yell and tilt his head up and we would have to lift the whole arrangement up to clear the chips out of the hole. We would keep this up until the auger punched right through to the other side. All this had to be done while the logs were floating; otherwise, if you drilled the holes in the log on dry land, you wouldn't know which way it would float once it got into the water, making it very difficult to chain two logs together. Balancing on one floating log while holding a gas-powered auger and drilling a hole in another floating log presented its own challenges, but at least we were wearing caulk boots to stay on the logs.

My stay with my dad in the logging camp was when I first put on caulk boots.

My father was quite a small man—maybe five feet six inches, if that, with very small feet. He had to have his caulk boots custom-made because they just did not regularly make size six caulk boots. Thus, at twelve I could fit into his boots, so I got to wear his spare pair. Boy, were they heavy, and very clunky on the feet.

Now with the logs sitting on the mud, he obviously couldn't move them, so he had to wait for the tide to come in. The whole estuary was tidal, so when the tide came in, it flooded, and once the tide came in enough, the logs floated, and then he had to shove them into deeper water where the stiff-legs were to form them into the log boom.

I had been running around on logs all my life, and it was awkward at first in the heavy boots, but most of the logs were very big around and stable in the water, so once I got on one, I could stay on it.

The technique was to balance on a log and then push against the bottom to get the log into deeper water, and then "stow" it in a row of other logs already there in the boom since the last tide. The logs often hung up on the bottom unless the tide was particularly high, so my dad would say, "Wait for the surge."

The mouth of the Nahwitti River was on the northeast side of Vancouver Island, facing Hope Island to the east and protected from the open ocean by the rest of northern Vancouver Island, but the remnants of large ocean swells still came up the river in periodic surges, so we would wait for a particularly large one to float stubborn logs into the pocket.

I have no idea how my dad did this himself, because he started relying on me right away even though I didn't understand what to do.

"Spread, spread," he yelled at me, without really explaining what or why I was doing anything. He just expected me to know what he was thinking.

Once a log was stowed between others, he wanted me to keep an opening between two more so he could move another one in.

The river water never stopped flowing to the sea, but the incoming tide and ocean surges would be attempting to push the logs back out of the stowing pocket as we pushed them in.

Once a tier of logs had been adequately stowed in place, he had "swifter" wire with dogs on it to drive into the logs to keep them from backing out. A dog is essentially a spike with a hole in it. The dogs were threaded on the wire like beads on a necklace, and key logs were spiked with the dogs to keep them from backing out of the boom.

The floating logs were mostly large and stable in the water, but some were smaller or low in the water and would start to sink a little bit if I stood on them.

Sometimes I had to run across a row of logs to make a spread for my dad coming along on a log from farther up the pocket.

I can't remember if I lost my balance or slipped on a piece of loose bark, but suddenly my feet went out from under me and I plunged feet-first into the water and, wearing no life jacket, immediately dropped to the bottom, standing there in six feet of water in my heavy caulk boots, screaming "Help!"

All that came out was bubbles, of course.

I was in the process of taking a breath and starting to drown when I felt something probing the back of my neck, and suddenly I was jerked off the bottom by the end of my father's pike pole. He dragged me out of the water onto a big log and I lay there, shaking and coughing out water, gasping for air.

"Jesus Christ, you scared the shit out of me," he said.

The old man (he was all of forty years old at the time) sent me ashore and back to camp to change clothes and take the rest of the day off.

That's when I hung around at the cookhouse.

The cook was a young guy who, as I'd heard privately when the men were talking, was allegedly gay. They claimed that he had learned to cook in prison, as if it were perfectly normal for homosexuals to be sent to prison. Homosexuality, or at least sodomy, was illegal in Canada until 1969. In any event, I overheard my dad telling another guy once that the cook had tried to kiss Magnus. Magnus was an ugly little Norwegian guy who had lost one leg in a logging accident back in Port Hardy and the O'Connors had hired to be camp manager. Trouble was that he wasn't management material. He had been a superb hooktender in the woods, but he was also an alcoholic and didn't know how to run a camp, so they eventually had to let him go.

The bunkhouses at Nahwitti were perched on the shore, just above the riverbank.
Rolf Leben photo

Like the cookhouse, which had a kitchen and seating at large tables for the whole crew, the bunkhouses were perched on the riverbank at the edge of the trees, a couple of them screened by huge spruce trees growing right out of the riverbank. One tree had half its roots undermined by the river and looked like it was ready to topple into the water at any time. The bunkhouses were a mix of small cabins stretched in a row from the cookhouse, all connected by a wooden sidewalk. The thick forest was right there behind the cabins, and the scent of the trees was heavy in the air.

The river flowed by right in front of the camp, the water level rising and falling with the tide. When you were going to sleep at night, you could hear the rush of the water going by just on the other side of the boardwalk.

I got to see something of Shorty around camp too. He was the bull cook, which meant that he did everything around camp but cook. He made the beds, washed the bedding and maybe men's clothes too (I can't remember), swept out the bunkhouses, maybe helped clean up in the cookhouse, and did some odd jobs around the living quarters if they needed doing.

Shorty's real name was Reginald Sagar. I asked him once what his surname meant and he explained that it had Viking origins. Of course, he had been in Canada a long time. Many, many years later, Joyce O'Connor told me she remembered when he came rowing up to her parents' float camp in Seymour Inlet in the 1940s.

He was not very tall, thus the nickname "Shorty," and he often had a red face, I remember, but of course that was usually in town when he had access to alcohol, for which he had a fondness. But then, most of my dad's friends seemed to have this habit.

I remember he often used the word *yegg* in conversation in much the same way other people would use the word *guy* when referring to a person. I had never and have never heard anyone one else use that word. It means "burglar" or "safecracker."

Shorty was also known as a very good watercolour painter, even though he didn't do it much. I think I saw one of his paintings once. It was delicate and detailed, if I recall correctly.

He also had a .303 Lee-Enfield rifle hanging over his bunk. He had painted it with glossy black paint, I remember. One time, it fell off the nails it was suspended on and went off. He had put it away loaded, with the expected consequences. Fortunately, everybody was at work when it happened. He eventually gave that rifle to my friend Kevin.

Sadly, I missed a significant event at camp. The oldest logger of them all, Nels the hooktender, was a Norwegian veteran high rigger. They were still using natural standing trees for spar trees at the O'Connor camp. They had finished working one hauling area or "side" and had moved to a new location, and Nels was going to climb the tallest sound tree in the setting, top it and rig it for hauling logs out. He was going to do it first thing the next morning, I was told, so all I had to do was get up with the rest of the crew, have breakfast and go out to the setting with the men.

I slept in.

The place was rumoured to have elk too, but I never saw one, even though the loggers said they had seen them at the very back end when they started logging. The Vancouver Island Roosevelt elk are known to be forest dwellers, unlike their cousins the Rocky Mountain elk. They are named for Theodore Roosevelt, who apparently had a fishing and hunting camp at Nahwitti.

There were still elk there a hundred years later. In 2000 I shot a 6x7 bull elk up in the headwaters of the Nahwitti River, off the road to Holberg.

Pretty soon it was time for the *Sea Logger* to come and tow the boom out to Port Hardy and I caught a ride back. Towing a log boom took a lot longer than the run up, so I had a lot of time to look at the rocky shoreline of Vancouver Island as we crawled along Goletas Channel.

Later that year there was an incident at camp involving a machine operator by the name of John Powell. He was diabetic—the first time I had ever heard of such a thing. We were seated at the dinner table in the cookhouse, and I saw a bottle of small white pills on the table. "What are those?" I asked my dad. He explained to me that they were saccharin tablets that John used to sweeten his coffee because as a diabetic he couldn't use sugar.

They took Sundays off in camp. Bored, John made himself a makeshift raft out of several planks over two empty forty-five-gallon drums and attempted to paddle across the flowing Nahwitti River in front of the camp. He was unable to reach the other side before he was swept out into Goletas Channel and disappeared. The radio telephone in camp failed to work, so my father jumped into his little Davidson skiff and rowed across Goletas Channel to the coast guard station in Bull Harbour on Hope Island to get help. Right in front of the mouth of the river is a notorious shallow stretch of water called Nahwitti Bar that has been known to sink fishing vessels crossing it at the wrong time of the tide. Somehow, the tide must have been in his favour, because my dad successfully rowed across and notified the coast guard, who dispatched a vessel to pick Johnny up.

The O'Connor company finished logging its claim at Nahwitti soon after and concentrated its operations in Port Hardy, logging up off the road to Holberg and at another isolated camp at Cleagh Creek on the west coast of the island. My father went to work in Holberg for several years after that and then ended up working for O'Connor again at their Port Hardy booming ground until he quit his logging career.

It was while my dad was working in camp in Holberg that I started hanging around with a kid I hadn't known before who was a little older than me but in the same grade.

He was one of those super-confident guys for whom everything seemed to be going right, and I started tagging along with him and hanging out at his place. He had a Beatles record and was fun to hang around with and told great stories, but what I didn't realize at the time was how much trouble he was going to get me into.

14 / **Thirteen and Trouble**

MY NEW FRIEND LIVED WITH his father and stepmother. An older brother and his mother lived in a city in the United States. He told me stories about all the amazing things his older brother did and how exciting life was when he went there. Even though it was a small farming city in eastern Washington State, he made it sound like the California we saw in movies like *Beach Blanket Bingo*, with beautiful girls, and guys driving cool hot rods and riding surfboards when they weren't smooching those bikini-clad beauties.

So I started hanging around this kid. He had that Beatles record, and his father had a couple of handguns that we used to play with. I think his stepmother considered herself something quite special. She was a tall redhead who drove around in a convertible like she was Elizabeth Taylor or something. She had a chrome-plated Smith and Wesson .38 calibre snub-nose revolver in her bedside table that my friend showed me and let me handle. I guess she figured she needed it to protect herself from all the men she imagined were watching when she drove by with the top down on her car.

Like several other men in Port Hardy, my friend's dad had a small trucking company, basically a gravel truck and a backhoe that he used to contract out on jobs with the local logging and construction companies. Even though he was still only fourteen, my friend said he knew how to drive. That turned out to be not necessarily a good thing.

I was getting frustrated and feeling hopeless in Port Hardy at thirteen. I couldn't imagine what kind of future I had there. I wasn't doing well in school in grade eight; I had had trouble with math since they introduced long division in grade three or four and subsequently fell behind in other subjects too. What was going to become of me? Would I end up being a logger for the rest of my life like some of the older boys who had quit school as soon as they were fifteen? The teachers at the school we attended never seemed to encourage any of us toward higher education. We were loggers' kids and Indigenous kids, and it was almost as if they didn't think we had the audacity or talent to achieve as exalted a position in our lives as they enjoyed with their two-year teaching certificate.

I was still in Scouts at the time but was rapidly losing interest. I had been really excited when two young single guys decided to start a Scout troop in Port Hardy two years before, but after the first year, one of them got killed in a logging accident, and when he suddenly wasn't there it wasn't so much fun anymore.

My friend was also in Scouts, and I found myself admiring him and following his lead no matter what he did.

One stunt we pulled had an economic impact on the whole town. I don't know how we managed to pull it off, but we agreed to sneak out of our homes in the middle of the night and go down to the logging camp. I don't think we even had plans, we just wanted to snoop around. But then we noticed that all the company pickup trucks at the shop—all the parked logging trucks, the fuel truck, lowbed trucks and everything else—had their keys left in the ignition. So we took the keys out of every vehicle we found them in.

Caused quite a kafuffle Monday morning when the men went to work and couldn't start any of the machines.

But the worst thing was that people would go grocery shopping on a Friday night, and if they were from Holberg or elsewhere out of town, they would go to the liquor store and stock up, then go to the beer parlour and have drinks before driving home on the narrow logging road after dark. And many of them wouldn't lock their car doors.

So my friend and I raided a car one time and stole a bunch of booze. There was a bottle of rum, some whisky and a bottle of Italian Chianti wine in that basket-shrouded bottle. We stashed them in a shed we had broken into near the hotel beer parlour.

Eventually, one night we both lied to our parents and said we were staying at each other's houses, or we just snuck out when we were supposed to be asleep, went to our hideout and started drinking. The object, of course, was to get drunk.

I can't remember what else we drank, but what I do clearly remember is that I wanted to try that Italian wine, but it had a cork in it. With no corkscrew, of course, we just smashed the neck of the bottle and drank from the jagged edge of the glass. It was harsh and sour stuff, but I persisted and chugged some down on top of the whisky or whatever else we had already drunk.

Eventually, we got totally drunk and started walking home. It was amazing that we didn't get seen by anyone, but it was already quite late in the evening. We walked up the hill past the community hall and the new Dong Chong supermarket, and at the crest of the hill right past the Anglican church was a small parking lot with some vehicles in it belonging to the gas station and car dealer across the street.

My friend decided to look inside an old pickup truck that was parked there and noticed that the keys were in the ignition.

"Hey, get in," he said, settling himself into the driver's seat. I struggled into the passenger seat without a second thought. What happened next changed my life forever. He started the truck, engaged the clutch and, despite claiming to know how to drive, lurched the truck out onto the gravel road and sped off down the straight stretch past the trailer home of a family we knew, past the school and down the hill, onto the straight stretch past Fisherman's Wharf, across the Glen Lyon River bridge, past my house where I was supposed to be asleep in bed, and past the logging camp where we had stolen all the keys not so long before that.

We got past the logging camp, and shortly afterwards, I don't know what happened, but he lost control of the truck and it turned sideways to the right and slammed into a rock face right beside the road, and I flew into the windshield, nearly going through it. Luckily, we didn't lose control to the left or we could have gone into the Quatse River.

I think the radiator was damaged, but he managed to get the truck into reverse, back up and turn back toward Port Hardy. He decided to return the truck. We should have just abandoned it, but an abandoned stolen truck and two drunk thirteen-year-olds wandering on the road would have been a dead giveaway too.

He had just parked the truck back in its spot opposite the car dealership when an RCMP vehicle pulled up on the road adjacent to us and a couple cops got out. I bailed out of the truck and tried to get away, but I was so drunk my whole body was just like rubber and the big burly cop collared me no problem.

I think I was violently puking as he dragged me to the back seat of the cop car.

When the cops brought me home and banged on the door, I think my parents were more saddened and disappointed than angry. That was the feeling I had about that incident for the rest of my life.

The next day, Sergeant Howk came and took a statement from me, promising that if I confessed to other crimes they wouldn't prosecute. So, hungover and contrite as I was, I gave him all the keys I had stolen from the logging company, plus a sawed-off .22-calibre rifle I'd bought off friends. They were common among fishermen to shoot large halibut and spring salmon in the head to calm them down before bringing them aboard. I never heard about those items again.

When I was brought before the magistrate, the wise old man, who was the timekeeper at the logging camp, asked me, "What am I going to do with you?"

"That's up to you," I replied. My parents visibly winced, as I was supposed to keep my mouth shut.

He gave me a one-year suspended sentence and warned me to stay out of trouble.

My parents arranged to send me away out of Port Hardy to live with an aunt and uncle in Montreal and go to a Catholic school for a year.

This was supposed to be punishment for me.

I went to Montreal in June 1967 with Expo 67 going full blast. I was exposed to the whole world in a nutshell at Expo 67, seeing the pavilions of all the various countries and modern art displays at the British and Youth pavilions, where I started meeting other young people who introduced me to the "scene" in downtown Montreal.

I started hanging around with the "summer hippies" at the Youth Pavilion, then with other, older hippies at a place called the Image on Pine Avenue in Montreal. Over my year there, I bought a guitar and, among other creative types, met a collective of people producing *Logos*, the English-language underground newspaper.

I returned to Port Hardy in August 1968, a reformed juvenile delinquent and now one of Port Hardy's first home-grown hippies. My parents didn't quite know what to make of this, but at least I wasn't stealing any more trucks.

My mother signed me up to the new Sea Cadets corps that was formed that first autumn I was back, but I was in there for only a few months. The haircuts, discipline and marching were not for me, even though I had gone to the captain and requested permission, as you do in the navy, to grow a beard, and he had agreed. I was fifteen and the only bearded Sea Cadet in Canada at that time.

After meeting the people back in Montreal who ran *Logos*, I had taken an interest in writing, I just didn't know what to write yet. The *North Island Gazette* advertised that they were looking for a high school correspondent, and I jumped at the chance. The *Gazette* also needed a hand putting the paper together, so I got a part-time job working in the office on weekends doing paste-up and editing raw copy from community correspondents. Working at the paper also gave me a closer insight into the political and industrial-commercial activities in the region. The Island Copper Mine was one of them.

15 / Island Copper

THE BIGGEST THING TO HIT Port Hardy in the time I lived there occurred during my high school years, and that was the establishment of the Island Copper Mine.

When career prospector Gordon Milbourne found a small piece of copper oxide under two windfall trees near Bay Lake, close to Rupert Inlet, in late 1965, he had no idea he was initiating a process that would create a mine producing 1.3 million tons of copper and turn Port Hardy from a sleepy village of 700 in 1969 to a bustling community of 4,500 people by 1974.

Milbourne had already staked four claims nearby in 1963 for the Empire Development Company, based on federal aerial magnetometer surveys. Digging two pits by hand at Bay Lake, he found more ore-grade material and staked the area. Several companies were offered the properties, but nothing came of discussions, Empire Development relinquished the claims, and they were turned over to Milbourne.

There had been prospecting in the area for many years, but renewed interest in copper in the area was sparked by the success of the Coast Copper Company's successful mine at Benson Lake.

Utah Construction and Mining took an interest in Milbourne's discoveries and took an option on the claims in 1966.

What followed was three years of extensive drilling and analysis of the claims, and in early 1969 Utah Construction and Mining decided to proceed with the mine. The one-page, three-word headline in the June 18 *North Island Gazette* declared "UTAH SAYS 'GO.' "

On December 2, 1970, after reading a notice in the *North Island Gazette* about an upcoming environmental hearing about the proposed open-pit copper mine out at Rupert Arm, near Port Hardy, I decided to skip school and hitchhike out to the airport to attend the hearing. I was sixteen at the time, and one of only sixteen members of the public to attend the hearing.

There had been attempts to develop mines on northern Vancouver Island ever since the first coal deposits on Vancouver Island were found near present-day Fort Rupert (the First Nations village of Tsaxis) in 1835. There was a gold mine at Zeballos in the 1930s and '40s and the productive mine at Benson Lake since 1962 (which closed in 1973). But the impact of that mine affected primarily the village of Port McNeill, and Port Hardy was still relatively immune to the economic impacts of a really big mine until Utah Mines got serious about the copper ore deposits at Rupert Inlet.

One thing about the Benson Lake mine that I learned in high school, though, was that sailors on the ore ships that docked at a place called Beach Camp, south of Port McNeill, used to sell my school chums something called "ocean whisky" and cigarettes they picked up cheap somewhere. I didn't hang around with those guys, so never had a drink of the stuff.

There had been lots of exploration on northern Vancouver Island over the years, so when the Utah Construction and Mining Company started drilling core samples at the Rupert Arm site and collecting them at a warehouse at the Port Hardy airport, few people except some eager local businessmen noticed. That was all about to change.

In fact, it had already started to change, even before the December environmental hearing into the application. Construction of the mine started in early 1970 before the public hearing and official approval occurred.

Port Hardy was shocked awake from its slumber as a minor coastal logging and fishing town turned into a mining boom town and it sank in that unlike many other "next big thing" predictions, this mine was really going to happen.

By early July there were 65 men employed in site preparation, and by the end of the month there were 270 men working on mill construction, and another 75 about to begin work on the company's residential subdivision in Port Hardy.

The company optimistically estimated at the time that there were 120 million tons of 0.5 percent copper in the ore body.

The public hearing had originally been planned for September, but was delayed until December 2, 1970. The hearing was in the drafty old barn of the former RCAF recreation centre out at the airport.

Because of technicalities, only four opponents to the mine were permitted to speak at the public hearing. Patrick Moore was one of them.

Moore, a twenty-three-year-old student at the time, was representing the Pacific Salmon Society and did his best to get Utah Construction and Mining to explain how dumping 9.3 million gallons of effluent daily into Rupert Inlet was not going to harm the marine ecosystem. Moore, who would write his PhD thesis on the pollution of Rupert Inlet by Utah Mines and go on to become president of Greenpeace, argued against a bank of company lawyers and mining science experts.

For his PhD, Moore researched heavy-metal contamination in Rupert Inlet by mine tailings. He concluded that existing mechanisms had failed to prevent unacceptable pollution.

In a story titled "Many Questions Left After Pollution Hearing" on page 6 of the December 9, 1970, *North Island Gazette*, the newspaper reported that "Almost single-handed a frail looking quiet-voiced 23-year-old student from Winter Harbour last Wednesday fought on behalf of the people of B.C., in a battle even he knew was lost before it began.

"Time after time at a hearing into Utah Construction and Mining Company's application for a permit to dump its Island Copper mine effluent into Rupert Arm, Patrick Moore forced the company's battery of experts into admissions that they really are not sure what effect the dumping will have on the inlet and rest of Quatsino sound."

But in a way, the hearing was almost like a Soviet show trial. The results had already been decided.

It didn't take long to get approval.

A headline in the January 28, 1971, edition of the *North Island Gazette* reported that "Utah Gets Dumping Permit—With Conditions."

With official approval, what everyone in Port Hardy knew already was confirmed. The mine and associated housing projects were going ahead.

Construction at the mine site and subdivisions planned for the anticipated flood of employees at the mine continued in a frenzied explosion of activity. Port Hardy's population peaked at five thousand at the height of the mine's operations. People from all over Canada and the rest of world came to Port Hardy, attracted by the mine. Some were career miners and others came to reinvent themselves. A former CBC television producer became a pump operator in the pit, and Pierre Trudeau's former Ottawa hairdresser ran a diamond drill.

At the peak of construction, more than five hundred people were engaged in building the mine site facilities, employee housing, water, power and sewer lines, and a road link to the Coal Harbour/Port Hardy Road.

The Seagate Hotel expanded in 1970, building a huge new

310-seat beer parlour and a 91-room addition to the hotel.

Already in 1969, the three-year-old municipality of Port Hardy had purchased seven hundred acres of land mostly for residential properties. When it was clear the mine was going ahead, the municipality sold over a hundred acres of land to Utah for a residential subdivision, with the company absorbing the cost of roads, water and sewage. Included in plans was a $600,000 recreation centre.

According to the book *The Story of Island Copper* by Craig Aspinall, by late 1974 Island Copper had built 292 houses, townhouses, duplexes and apartments in Port Hardy and had opened the 99-unit Highview Mobile Home Park. In 1975 the municipality added 97 housing lots close to the Island Copper subdivision and a mobile home park with 280 pads west of the company park. Shortly afterwards, 530 units of houses, condominiums and apartments were built on the former MacMillan Bloedel Ltd. site. In 1976 Island Copper added more homes in the new Park Drive subdivision. In 1979 private developers built two four-storey apartment buildings on land purchased from Utah. Fifty-two rental townhouse units were also built at the time.

A second large hotel in Port Hardy, the Thunderbird Inn, opened in 1973 with a large beer parlour and cocktail lounge. A giant shopping mall was created on a flat spot up behind the town.

Port Hardy's water and sewage facilities were inadequate for the population explosion, so Utah Mines funded dam work on the Tsulquate River, new trunk lines and two hundred-thousand-gallon storage tanks. Utah purchased $90,000 in municipal debentures, kick-starting construction of a $1.5 million sewage treatment plant.

Island Copper's mill and other buildings were incorporated into the municipality to expand the town's tax base. Island Copper's municipal tax bill for 1979 was $2,001,444.

After a hectic eleven months of mine and mill construction

following the official approval of the Island Copper Mine, the first shipment of ore—thirteen thousand tons of concentrate—left Rupert Inlet aboard the MS *Grimland* in December 1971.

The ore was mined in an open pit using truck-and-shovel methods. More than a billion tons of material was moved over the lifetime of the mine. At peak production in 1982, 170,800 tons were moved per day.

By the time mining concluded, the open pit was 7,900 feet long, 3,500 feet wide and 1,320 feet below sea level, making it the deepest excavation below sea level in the world.

By May 1995, six months before it shut down, Island Copper had produced 5.7 million tons of copper concentrate containing 1.3 million tons of copper, 1.1 million ounces of gold, and 11.6 million ounces of silver. The mine also produced 78,100 tons of molybdenum and 62,000 pounds of rhenium.

At its peak in 1980, Island Copper had a workforce of 900 men and women on the job, and 450 people were still working there right up until operations ceased.

The final blast in the pit occurred on July 31, 1995, and the last rock went into the crusher at noon on August 2, 1995, and then Island Copper had finished mining, but Port Hardy was never the same.

Neither was the inlet or the mine site. Excavated waste rock was dumped into the inlet, creating 640 acres of land, with some other waste dumped outside the pit. Tailings from the mill were dumped into the inlet through a submarine tailings disposal system.

In a 2012 paper, Patrick Moore, once the greatest critic of Island Copper's underwater disposal of mine tailings, joined former Island Copper biologists Clem Pelletier and Ian Horne to conclude that the underwater disposal had no negative effects.

"It can be stated with reasonable confidence that one year after closure of the Island Copper Mine there is no evidence of any significant environmental or economic damage as a result of submarine tailings disposal," they wrote. "It can be concluded, with certainty, that recolonization of the marine environment has and is occurring at a rapid rate. There has been some modification of habitat, in some areas, from rocky to sandy bottom, but the new habitat is healthy and colonized with marine life." The pit was flooded with sea water to become a lake.

***

Even though the mine was hiring in June 1971, when I graduated from high school, I had plenty of other things on my mind than getting a job there. I was deep into a serious relationship with my girlfriend, who was leaving for Europe as soon as she could save enough money, so I knew I'd have to get some money together quickly if I wanted to follow her to Europe later in the year.

Fortunately, I knew my dad would hire me at the O'Connor Logging booming ground as soon as I finished school, because that was right around the same time of year that his regular boom man, Henry George from Tsulquate, would quit to go gillnetting salmon for the summer.

But before I finished high school I had to satisfy a serious itch that had been bugging me for years. I had to hike to Cape Scott.

16 / Alone to Cape Scott

THE SKY GOT EVEN DARKER under the thick canopy of trees, and snow started falling in heavy, wet flakes as I continued to trudge along in the mud of the Cape Scott Trail with my heavy pack on my back. After a nearly sleepless night curled up on the operator's seat of a spar tree in the middle of a clear-cut and a full day hiking the muddy trail, I was approaching exhaustion. I was soaked to the skin from sweat and rain and muddy up to my crotch despite my rain gear, and if I didn't find shelter for the night, I was in danger of getting hypothermia.

Suddenly, the forest came to an end, and I entered a wide meadow fringed by trees, and through the screen of falling snow, there in the middle of the meadow was a big old farmhouse with white smoke coming out of the chimney. I could hardly believe it.

I don't know when I first heard of Cape Scott. It seemed as if I always kind of knew that there were the remains of an old settlement at the very northern tip of Vancouver Island, but when I was very young, I didn't realize that there was a trail all the way there from Holberg.

My father told me that in the autumn of 1958 he and a friend of his chartered a float plane and got themselves dropped off at Hansen Lagoon, a part of the old Danish settlement at Cape Scott. When the Danes went there to settle in 1896, one of the large tasks they undertook was to tame the wild meadows of salt marsh at the head of four-mile-long Hansen Lagoon, dike and fence it and use it to grow hay. They built over a mile of dike to keep the ocean out. The Danes built homes and had farms inland of Hansen Lagoon as well, but the lack of a harbour, foul weather, and no market for their beef and produce effectively killed the original settlement by 1909. Others attempted to settle there, but by the early 1950s it was abandoned by almost everyone.

Now and then over the years as I was growing up, my father would mention that he and his friend had stayed in the "Spencer house" that was just a short way up a trail from the head of the lagoon. It was a large, well-built family home, he recalled. The place looked like it had only been vacated, he told me years later, with most of the family's furnishings still in place and intact, and a note on the door saying that people were welcome and to please close the door when they left. The place had been the official post office for the Cape Scott settlement and in fact operated until 1943.

Alfred Spencer lived in the house from 1912 to 1958.

My friend John Lyon visited it in 1960 while fishing with his father. They anchored in and he went ashore.

"When I walked into this house from where my dad had anchored in Fisherman's Bay back in 1960, I found a calendar from 1958, a hand-crank telephone and a wooden, hand-cranked washing machine with kind of a spinning tub, with fins sticking out from the sides on the inside to make sure the clothes got properly thrashed about," he told me years later. "The house seemed ready for someone to move back in. The front porch was sinking, though."

It was also well-known around Port Hardy that the Royal Canadian Air Force had a radar base at Cape Scott during the war, as part of a chain of radar stations for surveillance of the Canadian and American coast. The Cape Scott station, officially known as 10 Radio Unit (RU) Cape Scott, became operational on February 5, 1943, and was officially disbanded in 1945. At its height, the station housed seventy men on two sites: the actual radar site at the Cape and a second residential campsite.

It was Easter weekend, 1971. I was in my last year at North Island Secondary School and had developed a real desire to see Cape Scott. Some friends in Port Hardy had hiked up the year before and I felt like I was really missing out on something. There were very few if any real trails that you could hike on northern Vancouver Island at the time and the Cape Scott Trail was the most exciting one of all.

The trail originally started right at the edge of the village of Holberg, and in World War II it had been accessible by a rough jeep road as far as settler Bernt Ronning's homestead, where the actual walking trail started.

Subsequent logging had obliterated the trail and intersected it in numerous places, and there was now a parking lot up off one of the logging roads where the trail to San Josef Bay and Cape Scott started. San Josef Bay was two miles from the parking lot, and Cape Scott itself was fourteen and a half miles from the trailhead. Hansen Lagoon, where I knew there was a cabin on the beach, was nine miles from the trailhead.

I had been to San Josef Bay once before, just that previous October, with my girlfriend Pam, camping out on the ground in an old shack with no door.

I knew that the students from Holberg and the air force radar base there, who lived in the student dormitory in Port McNeill, caught a bus home on weekends, so I brought my pack full of my sleeping bag and food and rain gear and caulk boots along to school on the Thursday morning before Good Friday.

Thursday afternoon, April 8, when classes were over, I joined the Holberg kids for the ride to Holberg. I was familiar with the winding logging road to the other side of the island from Port Hardy because I had been hunting for several years with my dad up in the meadows on the other side of Kains Lake, which was about nine and one-half miles up the road from Port Hardy.

In the logging camp of Holberg itself, the bus driver dropped off the students living in family housing there and then proceeded out toward Canadian Forces Station Holberg, three and a half miles north. The actual radar tracking site was on nearby Mount Brandes. The base was the westernmost station of the Pinetree Line, forty-four radar stations established across Canada during the Cold War. Construction of the base started in 1950, and it became operational in 1954. The base closed in 1990.

When the bus came to the "Elephant Crossing," I signalled to the driver, and he dropped me off. The Elephant Crossing was where the road out to the base crossed the San Josef Main logging road. Air force men new to Holberg had never seen big West Coast logging trucks before, and when they saw the big Hayes and Kenworth logging trucks heading back to the woods empty, with their rear section mounted on top of the front and the long reach of the trailer projecting over the cab of the truck, they thought of elephants. The name stuck and there was even a sign now at the junction saying "Elephant Crossing."

I now had to walk the rest of the way to Cape Scott unless someone in a vehicle might be heading out that way. But I had no such luck. By the time I had disembarked from the bus, hefted my pack onto my back and started trekking, the logging trucks had finished hauling from the woods for the day and no more were heading out the main. They probably weren't allowed to pick up passengers anyway. A couple of management stragglers came roaring out of the woods in their muddy company trucks, but there was no traffic heading toward the Cape Scott Trail parking lot.

I kept walking. Fortunately, it wasn't raining, or only raining lightly. I just kept walking.

Dusk was rapidly approaching, and I started to wonder what I was going to do for shelter for the night. All I had was a Canadian army-surplus poncho. No tent. By now it was really starting to get dark. What was I going to do?

I rounded a corner on the logging road and there, almost as if it had been conjured up especially for me, was a spar tree standing in a wide-open, flat area just a couple hundred yards off the main road. I walked down the spur road, dropped my pack at the base of the tall steel log-hauling tower and climbed up to the cab. Thankfully, the door was unlocked. I swung it open. It was cold inside and stank of cigarette smoke. All it had was a single bucket seat with worn plastic upholstery, but I wasn't expecting a queen-size bed in there. It was shelter. I climbed down for my backpack and, sitting in the operator's chair, squeezed it in between my legs and closed the door.

It was kind of odd that they were logging so close to the road and still so close to Holberg. I thought that they would have taken all the easy, good wood first as they had started logging around Holberg in the 1920s. Maybe there was a good stand of old-growth spruce or cedar that they had just never got around to. Either way, I was delighted to find the spar tree.

I must have had some kind of food with me, because by now I was hungry, so I must have eaten something. Now it was completely dark outside and cold in the cab, so I dug my sleeping bag out and wrapped it around me and tried to figure out how I could sleep sitting up in the cramped seat. I had just figured out how to stretch my legs at an angle around the foot pedals of the machine when the black night was illuminated by a great flash of lightning that lit up the whole clear-cut around me, followed by the loud crack of what sounded like a thunderhead right above me.

Shit! Here I was, in the only standing thing in a broad clear-cut and it was all made of steel with an eighty-foot steel tower sticking up in the air to attract the lightning. All I could do was pull my legs up off the floor, make sure I didn't touch any of the metal in the cab, curl up as best I could on the seat of the machine and hope that I wouldn't get struck by lightning. I'd rarely experienced thunder and lightning storms on northern Vancouver Island. Why did this one have to happen when I was inside a steel spar tree for what was the first and probably only time in my life? It wasn't fair.

At least I could kind of rest my feet on top of my backpack, so I didn't have to remain curled up like a hamster all night. The storm passed and it started raining heavily, drumming on the roof of the cab of the machine, but the lightning never struck again. It was as if it had just been a one-off, freak event.

I tried to sleep, but I remember being awake more than asleep that night. I can't even say I tossed and turned because there was no room. I must have dozed off finally, because at one point I woke up and dawn was breaking.

I unwrapped my sleeping bag from around me, stowed it away in the pack and, trying to straighten myself out, opened the door of the cab and climbed down the ladder, taking my pack with me.

Down on the ground again, it was time to continue the trek to Cape Scott.

If I had any hope of catching a ride to the trailhead with a company foreman or mechanic or any kind of logging company traffic, I was out of luck. It was Good Friday, and the camp must have shut down for the long weekend. As in the evening before, on my walk from the Elephant Crossing, no traffic came along, and I had to walk the rest of the way on the gravel logging road to the rough parking lot at the trailhead.

The road bypassed the few remaining settlers' cabins which lined the trail when last I was here. Bernt Ronning's place was the most remarkable, with a huge monkey-puzzle (*Araucaria araucana*) tree growing in front of it. He had been well-known for collecting exotic plants from around the world.

The only original settler I ever met was a former American,

Mr. Lincoln, who gave Pam and me a hand-drawn map of the trail that he had had photocopied to hand out to hikers.

He lived in a small, shingled house, as did several other old bachelors there, like Willie Hecht and Jim Cordy.

We dropped in and were welcomed with a cup of tea and a chat, and Mr. Lincoln gave me the map with notes on whose cabin was along the way, the turnoff to San Josef Bay, the side trails to Guise Bay and other sights. It was like a hobbit map, with little notes and sketches included.

I kept that map for years, but it got wet and folded so many times it was a mere scrap of paper the last time I saw it.

According to the Port Hardy Museum, Earle R. Lincoln was an MIT-educated scholar who arrived in the 1930s and took menial jobs during the Depression. Lincoln kept a meticulous ledger that included lists of every possession he owned, including an extensive book collection, as well as cards and gifts he had sent and received, and work performed, with columns noting the employer, the dates, job duties (ditch digging was a recurring notation) and payment.

When Mr. Lincoln died, his possessions were scattered among the Holberg community, including his .30-30 Winchester rifle. The fellow who got it owed my father some money and traded it to him in lieu of payment. I own that rifle now and will donate it to the Port Hardy Museum to add to the other personal effects of Mr. Lincoln on display.

The first two-mile stretch to the San Josef Bay turnoff was pretty well maintained, and despite my nearly sleepless night in the cab of the steel spar and the already long walk up the logging road to the trailhead, I was energized and excited to be finally on my way to Cape Scott.

I might even run into the mysterious Jim Smith, who friends of mine said lived along the trail somewhere. He was an American draft dodger who had taken to living in the woods somewhere between Holberg and Cape Scott and apparently had painstakingly wound up and coiled the copper telephone wire that remained parallel to the trail after the collapse of the settlement.

What followed next was a long, hard slog through the mud. Immediately after the junction, the trail became much rougher. It headed slightly uphill and became very wet and slippery over sections of old corduroy road.

The next two hours introduced me to the real Cape Scott Trail. It is a very wet climate there, and though there were dry parts of the trail when it skirted a hillside, often it was muddy, very muddy. Sometimes there were dry sections that I could kind of walk on to get through the wet parts, sometimes I just had to plough through the mud, other times there were exposed roots I could walk on, and sometimes logs or broken branches had been tossed into the muck to make paths through.

There were fallen trees across the trail in many places as well. Some were old windfalls and high enough from bank to bank that you could kind of duck under them. But others were freshly knocked down by the winter storms, with thick branches completely blocking the trail, so I had to take my pack off and fight my way though the branches and climb over or under the tree trunk.

I got into a rhythm, and for some stupid reason I kept thinking back to a Rudyard Kipling poem with a refrain I thought went "We're foot, slog slogging, slogging our way to India," and kept repeating that to myself as I trudged along.

It turns out that the phrase is from a poem called "Boots" and actually goes like this:

We're foot–slog–slog–slog—slogging over Africa—
Foot–foot–foot–foot—slogging over Africa—
(Boots–boots–boots–boots—moving up and down again!)
There' s no discharge in the war!

But I didn't know that at the time, and it set up a rhythm that helped me to keep going even though I was tired already.

At around three miles along the trail, the forest changed from thick old-growth to spindly trees in a more open and boggy area. The trail now followed a long, straight section of the old corduroy road. There were still remnants of old drainage ditches on either side.

After at least three hours, probably more considering the mud, I finally came to the Fisherman River bordered by big old-growth trees.

Luckily, as there was no real bridge across the river, a giant spruce tree had fallen over right at the trail, making a natural crossing. I walked across the thick log, noticing a sewing machine stand half-buried in the sand. Once across, I found a place to sit down and take off my pack to catch my breath and prepare for the next stretch to Hansen Lagoon, though I didn't know how long that was going to take me. I was already wondering where I was going to sleep that night if I didn't make it to the air force cabin at the mouth of this same Fisherman River, but who knows how many hours it would take to get to the mouth?

Finally, I had to get up and get going. My back was still wet under my clothes, and the press of the heavy pack on the cold cloth on my back made me wince at first, but it warmed up once I started hiking again. If I thought that the first part of the trail had been tough, the next part would be even tougher.

The thick forest of old-growth trees along the Fisherman River petered out, and the trail passed though a boggy area dominated by small, stunted trees with water running everywhere, particularly onto the trail, creating one mud hole after another.

Some of the mud holes, like others on the way to Fisherman River, were shallow enough that I could wade through them, and at other times there were dry edges on the main path that I could step onto and skirt around the mucky part.

One time a mud hole didn't look that bad or wet, but it was deceptive. I took one step into it and sank up to my knees, with one leg and then the other planting even deeper as I tried to regain my balance, and then fell face-first into the mud with my pack on my back pressing me down. I extended my arms, of course, plunging them shoulder deep into the cold, wet, clammy muck as well. I had to roll to my side to try to extract myself from this quagmire and by the time I did I was covered head to toe with the stuff.

The trail didn't improve as the day wore on. It had been raining since I left the Fisherman River, and the day was wearing on too. I didn't have a watch, but I could tell even in the thick cover of the virgin forest on both sides of the trail that it was getting later in the day.

As I hiked along, there were more windfall trees across the trail to climb through, over or under, and in some places the salal and salmonberry bushes grew so thickly that they encroached on the trail too.

I was grateful that at least I had decided to wear my rubber caulk boots, which I wore when I was working on weekends with my father on the log boom in Port Hardy. They gave me traction on the roots of the trees on both sides of the path, both the exposed ones and those hidden under the muck. But by now, even with my army poncho and logger's rain pants, I was soaked. The mud had even climbed up inside my rain pants and I could feel it soaking my pants above my boots.

The trail had reached a kind of plateau now, passing through a semi-alpine area of bog land with small and dead or dying trees.

It was starting to feel like this trail would never end. Even repeating the Kipling marching song over and over again didn't inspire me anymore. I wasn't out of breath, I couldn't go fast enough for that, but my legs and back were starting to feel the effects of struggling across the mud and obstacles with the weight of my pack. Even the slightest incline uphill was starting to feel like a major climb.

The boggy area finally came to an end, and I re-entered a forest of taller trees.

Even though it was April 10 now and the days were getting longer, as I trudged along for what must have been two hours past the Fisherman River, judging by the fading light, it seemed as if it was evening. There had been a steady drizzle all day, and that miraculously stopped around the same time that the small patch of sky between the thick trees got darker and darker.

The trail levelled out and the walking was finally a little bit easier. It was a relief on the legs not to have to wade through more mud or clamber through more fallen trees, even if it was for a moment. I was wet now, though, tired and hungry, and was seriously worrying where the heck I was going to spend the night if I didn't make it all the way to the cabin in Hansen Lagoon.

The terrain changed too. Having left the thick forest on both sides of the trail, I was now in an area of small natural meadows mixed with stands of smaller trees. It was a lot like the semi-alpine area on the other side of Kains Lake off the Holberg road, where I hunted with my dad in the fall.

I passed the low collapsed remains of someone's log house. I came to a junction in the trail with a notice that Nels Bight was straight ahead. I took the left-hand turn heading downhill through the trees toward Hansen Lagoon.

Suddenly, from one moment to the next, the trail emerged out of the trees. I stepped out into a broad clearing at the same moment that the sky opened and started shedding enormous, wet snowflakes. There, through the curtain of falling snow in the middle of the wide meadow fringed all around by the trees, I saw a solid, square house with a four-sided peaked roof and white smoke coming out of the chimney. I could not believe it.

I approached the house, the snow accumulating on me as I walked the several hundred yards toward it and around to the other side to find the entrance. The porch was long gone, but someone had piled up some logs and other debris, probably from a nearby fallen barn, for elevation to get into the open doorway. The door was not there anymore either.

The inside of the main floor was completely bare except for a dismantled and rusty stove, so that wasn't the source of the smoke, and there was no sign of anyone, so whoever was in the house with a fire going must be upstairs, I figured. There was a bare set of stairs up to the next floor, so I walked up, calling as I went. "Hey, anybody home?"

"Yeah, up here," came a voice from above the stairs. I climbed the rest of the way up and as soon as my head breached the top I saw three people in a semicircle in front of a fireplace crackling with a bright fire.

It was an adult and two young teenagers. It looked like they had not been there long either. They had taken off some of their wet outer clothing and were holding it up toward the flames to dry it out.

They introduced themselves, and even though they didn't come out and specifically say it out loud, I kind of got the impression that he was a social worker and they were a couple of kids being taken on an Outward Bound kind of program to show them some outdoor and self-reliance skills.

The insides of the whole upstairs of the house had been gutted. The sheathing on the inside walls had been mostly pulled off for firewood. I suppose these guys were burning some sticks from outside, but they too were using parts of the inside of the house for the fire.

I was kind of wondering how the chimney could still be working after all these years. After all, my dad had told me the place was empty when he was there in 1958, thirteen years before me. And how was the chimney connected to the disconnected stove downstairs?

Either way, I wasn't too concerned. It seemed safe enough and I was so tired, cold and hungry that I was grateful for the shelter and the warmth. I must have had some food along and a way to heat it up or cook it, but that is something I do not remember at all from that trip.

I didn't have a blue foam pad or Thermarest—that kind of thing wasn't available yet. So I slept on the bare wooden floor as close to the fireplace as I could with those three other guys there already. At least most of the floor was still intact.

By morning the snow had stopped and it had warmed up, leaving only a few patches of snow here and there on the ground.

After a short downhill walk, I emerged out of the trees at the head of Hansen Lagoon, which stretched out in front of me like a large, grassy meadow surrounded by low wooded hills on both sides.

As soon as I got down to the lagoon, I saw why the original Danish settlers thought that it was good place to rear cattle. Except for the low, wooded hills, it looked more like part of the Prairies than some place on the BC coast. It must have been at least half a mile across and looking out toward the ocean, which wasn't visible—the tall grass looked like it just went on and on.

I knew that the air force cabin was somewhere to my left along the edge of Hansen Lagoon, at the mouth of the Fisherman River, the same river that I had crossed on the log bridge the day before. But how to traverse all this grass?

There was a trampled path to the left toward the trees, so I started walking on that. As I was walking along though, I came across deep ditches in the ground I had to jump across, which was barely manageable with a big pack on. Finally, after some manoeuvring, I was able to get to the edge of the timber where it met the grassy meadow and then started walking along the edge toward the river.

Looking out over the meadow and the fallen grass from the year before, I saw two lines of fence posts, still there after sixty years, weathered and grey but still standing in a neat row on each side of a deep, ruler-straight ditch. If only they could talk and tell the story of the brave pioneers who had so carefully dug that ditch

Sixty years later, the fence posts that settlers had put in at Hansen Lagoon were still intact. I wore an army surplus rain poncho, rain pants and rubber caulk boots to hike to Cape Scott. *Author's collection*

in an effort to keep the marshes drained to graze their cattle.

Skirting along the edge of the trees, I could see that the tide was out right now, but looking out I could see a network of narrow channels snaking along in the marsh that the tidewater would fill before flooding the tidal marsh. It would be harder to navigate along here when the tide was all the way in.

The air was different here. Inland on the main trail, the scent was all forest and tree needles, but the salt marsh had a skunky, fermented, muddy scent mixed with the salt air blowing in from the open ocean.

I weaved my way along the shore toward the Fisherman River. Sometimes it was easier to follow the trees along the shore and at other times it was easier to head down to the marsh that remained at the shore's edge between the trees and the mud flats and walk on the hummocks poking up above the little trenches that the water made while flowing from the land to the sea and back again.

After carefully negotiating my way along every easy route

I could find, finally ahead of me on the shore I could see a wide, flat area with water flowing out to the sea. That must be the Fisherman River.

I kept walking along and sure enough, as I got closer and could look upstream, there was a good strong stream of water pouring out of the river, and there on the bank to my left was a substantial cabin. To my surprise, just like the last lonely building I had come across, this one had smoke coming out of the chimney. Two people were walking around outside the cabin as well, so I approached them and said hello.

As I got closer, I realized they were two people I knew from Port Hardy, Tom and Trish, and when they heard us talking outside, two more people came and looked out the door of the cabin. They were Paul and Leslie, another couple from Port Hardy. Wow. This was turning out to be quite a gang.

I walked up to the cabin, dropped my heavy pack and had a look inside. It was a basic plywood-wall building with a set of bunks along one wall and across one end of the large single room. It had a good cook stove in it and a food preparation counter with shelving for food storage as well.

Looking around the room, I didn't take long to see a big hole in one corner, dotted with shotgun pellet marks around the outside of it. Someone had discharged a shotgun in here at one point, probably at a rat.

I had barely settled in and had a cup of tea thick with honey and a bite to eat when Tom suddenly said, "We're going upriver to go see Julia, do you want to come?"

I had heard about this couple Ron and Julia, who were living up there up there in a cabin they had built. That sounded like a great idea, so I agreed.

Tom led the way. He had a big red spot on one nostril from getting snagged by a fish hook the day before. It looked angry and inflamed, but they were treating it as best they could with whatever minimal first-aid equipment they had brought along.

We walked out onto the estuary of the river before attempting to cross it. It was way too deep in front of the cabin. Even out on the estuary, where we tried to find the flattest part to cross, we ended up going in over the top of our boots. There is nothing quite like that sensation of having cold water rush in over your boots and soak your feet, and then walking along through the water with the squishy-squish feeling in your boots as your wet socks and insoles slosh around in there.

Once we got to the other side, we all sat down and pulled our boots off and wrung our socks and insoles out as best we could.

Now dried out and ready to go, we looked for the trail up to Ron and Julia's cabin. It was supposed to follow the edge of the river up into the hills above Hansen Lagoon. It didn't take long to find the footpath going upriver. The trees down at the ocean's edge were taller; then, as we hiked further inland, they got slightly smaller. It was a mixed coastal forest of cedars, many of them with dead grey tops that we called "spike-top cedars" mixed with the usual coastal hemlock and spruce, as well as some yellow cedar. Both sides of the trail were thick with salal and mixed huckleberry and blueberry bushes. It wasn't hard to follow the path, as it was obvious people had occasionally used it.

The scent in the air was a perfume blending all the fragrances of the various evergreen trees into its very own blend that filled the nostrils and lungs like nothing else.

Once in a while I would brush against a yellow cedar branch and immediately get sent back to the forest on the other side of Vancouver Island.

The trail skirted into the forest and away from the river, meandering in the flat, alpine-like terrain, then swung back toward the river. We could hear the ripple of the river once again and smelled wood smoke just before we came into a clearing right near the banks of the river, and then came to Ron and

Julia's cabin.

It was a freshly built hexagon of cedar logs, glowing almost bright yellow, with a cedar post at each corner of the hexagon and short logs stacked one on top of the other for walls. Three of the walls were of solid logs all the way to the roof, but the front three walls only came up about four feet high and the rest of the space was filled with stretched construction plastic. The roof also glowed, reddish brown this time from the freshly split shakes.

We made some noise as we approached, so as not to frighten Julia. Julia came to the door when we called and opened it. She was a slight, blond-haired woman with the bangs cut high on her forehead. She greeted us and invited us in.

We apologized for the muddy boots and wet socks, but she let us take our boots off in the entrance to the cabin and come inside in our wet socks.

It was warm and cozy inside from the heat coming off the airtight wood stove. It would have been a major task to carry that stove up the Cape Scott Trail all the way from Holberg.

While we were there, though, over tea, Julia told us how to find the shortcut down from the Fisherman River bridge to the cabin and Hansen Lagoon.

The inside of the six-sided cabin was very welcoming. It was one space, so it was nice and airy. Ron and Julia had their bed against the back wall, and a wide counter ran around the inside of the cabin. On the floor under the counter were large metal cannisters where they kept dried foodstuffs, I supposed.

The table and chairs were homemade, as was the front door, milled from a log with a chainsaw, as far as I could tell from the chainsaw marks on the boards.

Ron was away at the time, in Holberg on some kind of business or away at a lighthouse. I think Ron and Julia had got into relief lighthouse keeping after meeting the keepers at the Cape Scott light.

It was one way to maintain their lifestyle in the cabin on the

Fisherman River and get cash employment at the same time.

Living off the land is a wonderful concept, but eventually you realize that you cannot grow coffee, power-saw gas or flour and sugar.

It was light and bright inside the cabin, but Julia explained that they had plans to get real glass windows to replace the opaque plastic, and how they would have to plan ahead to order a whole bargeload or at least a boatload of building supplies to be delivered to the shore of Hansen Lagoon. I'll bet she had hopes of getting a real wood stove too. An airtight was good enough for heat, but if you were living in a cabin like that all year round, it would be better to have a stove with a real cooking surface and an oven to bake in, I'm sure.

While we were there, Julia mentioned that she and Ron were not the only ones on the property. They were partners with a couple named Doug and Kyoko, who had built their cabin across the river and upstream about half a mile from Ron and Julia.

Ron and Julia's land ended up getting expropriated when the area was declared a provincial park in 1973.

I had no idea then, as I was seventeen years old and single, but only four years later, in 1975, I would be back there and staying in that cabin with my new wife Juliane and mother-in-law. Ron and Julia had left the cabin fully intact and full of food and supplies, so we were very comfortable.

Pretty soon it was time to head back, so we said goodbye to Julia.

Back at the cabin, Tom decided to go down to the riverbank to try fishing again, only without catching his nose this time, and Paul and I set off into the woods behind the cabin to try to find enough firewood for the night.

When we got back with armfuls of windfall sticks and branches, as there was an axe at the cabin but no saw to cut lengths off logs with, another person had arrived.

He said his name was Graham, and that he was the junior

keeper at the Cape Scott lighthouse. He was on his day off and had decided to hike over to the Fisherman River to try his hand at some trout fishing. We had a brief chat and he went fishing, but not before extending an invitation to drop in at the light station for a visit.

The next day, April 12, we decided to head out for the cape. It had been a nice break at the air force cabin after my forced march up the trail from the Elephant Crossing to Spencer's house, but I was ready to get going. I had yet to see the beaches of that end of the island and was looking forward to that.

Paul and Leslie decided to stay another night at the air force cabin, and said they'd come with us for the hike to the cape. Tom said he knew of a place to stay on the way there, at the sand neck, and when I asked, he said there'd be room for me too.

Having made the trip in once, we found it pretty easy to make our way through the marsh grass back to the head of the lagoon where the trail emerged from Spencer's house and rejoined the Cape Scott Trail. From there, it was an easy hike for the approximately half a mile over to Nels Bight, effectively crossing over from one side of Vancouver Island to the other.

Even before we got there, we could hear the sound of the ocean's waves through the trees and smell the scent of churned-up salt water on the wind.

Emerging from the trail through the trees, we came to a huge tangle of logs piled high on the beach by the high tides and wind, the oldest ones grey and weathered, with new, freshly washed-up logs brown and reddish from bashing up on the beach and against other logs.

All we could see was white sandy beach spreading for two miles, facing northwest.

Scrambling across the logs, we got down onto the exposed sand, as the tide was still only half-out, and then walked about half a mile along the sandy beach before reaching the continuation of the trail into the bush. That part of the trail ran another two miles through the stunted coastal forest and emerged onto another lovely off-white beach at Experiment Bight.

The crazy thing about Experiment Bight was the sand dunes at the western end of the beach that continued all the way across the island for several hundred yards before reaching Guise Bay, facing south on the other side of the island.

Tom said he wanted to show us the cabin at Guise Bay, so he led us through a gap in the bush to the remains of a plank road and, nearby, a tiny little cabin made of interlocking two-by-six planks. It was the last remaining structure from the World War II radar base.

Inside, it was obvious someone had recently been living there. There was even a bed, or a bed frame at least, with springs and no mattress.

After we stashed our packs in the cabin, we set out for Cape Scott.

There were still a few fence posts standing at the edge of the sand neck. Back in the days of the settlement, someone had tried to farm here too, but the wind blowing from the ocean kept eroding the topsoil, and that was why it was just a small desert from one side of the island to the other here.

From the sand neck at Guise Bay to the Cape Scott light station was about another two miles, first through some thick forest. Then the old plank road left over from the radar base appeared under our feet, with most of the planks long gone and only the cross members underneath remaining. Moss and ferns were doing their best to reclaim the forest floor.

Shortly before the light station the old plank road turned into a gravel road, and then we were at the lighthouse buildings.

The light station was your typical British Columbia lighthouse; white buildings with red roofs and everything licked clean as if the Queen herself was coming to visit. There were two main dwellings for the light keepers, one for the senior keeper and one for the junior keeper, and two larger outbuildings, plus a smaller one. The light itself was on a short steel tower just past the buildings, where it could be seen from most angles out at sea. The array of horns was set up near a small powerhouse with the horns facing several different directions.

After a short walk from the lighthouse building on a well-maintained narrow path, we came to a bare-rock outcropping that dropped off to swirling sea water below. A precarious-looking steel-wire suspension bridge swung out over the crashing waves rushing right through the narrow gorge below us, from the outside of Vancouver Island to the other side.

One by one we crossed the narrow, swinging bridge over the swirling water.

If we thought the breeze was fresh when it was blowing in from the ocean back at the sand neck, that was really just a breeze. After climbing off the bridge and walking out on the bare rock promontory that was the actual Cape Scott, we were blasted by a stiff onshore wind rushing in from the Pacific Ocean.

There was now nothing between us and Asia but thousands and thousands of miles of salt water. It was not even stormy by any means, but still huge rollers rolled in from the open Pacific, turning into breaking waves as they crashed into the west side of the cape.

Amazingly, there were beds of kelp clinging to the bottom all around the base of the cape, particularly on the east side opposite from where the waves from the west were perpetually hammering. A lone sea lion surfaced and dived just outside the beds of kelp, and seagulls coasted and windsurfed in the wind. Now it was almost as if we were breathing compressed air into our lungs.

"Just think, if you were to head straight across, you wouldn't see land until you got to Japan," Tom said.

I disagreed, stating that I looked it up once and determined that technically, if you went straight across the ocean from Cape Scott, you would arrive at the southern end of the Kamchatka Peninsula.

We had no way of proving it one way or the other, so we turned around and, after crossing the swinging bridge one by one again, hiked back to the lighthouse building and along the trail back to the sand neck.

From the sand neck, Paul and Leslie headed back to Hansen Lagoon, and Tom and Trish and I went exploring over the dunes to the beach at Experiment Bight.

That night, Tom and Trish took the bed and I slept on the floor, which wasn't the most pleasant of situations because the place already had other occupants on whose territory we were squatting: rats. I could hear them skittering along the floor and feel them run across my sleeping bag. It was a little disconcerting, and on the hard wooden floor with no mat under me, it wasn't the most comfortable night's sleep I had ever had.

After Tom and Trish left, I tried out the bed, rolling my sleeping bag out onto it. It wouldn't be as comfortable as a mattress on a bed, but my next night was going to be a lot more comfortable than the one on the floor with the rats, that was for sure. The rats might even stay on the floor. Looking through the springs of the bed, I thought I saw something long and dark shoved up against the wall and squinted down to peek through the springs. Looked like a rifle.

I crawled under the bed and retrieved it.

It was a pretty damn nice rifle, a short Lee-Enfield "Jungle carbine," as it was popularly called. This one was still in pretty good shape; it had been well-oiled and taken care of before being left in the cabin. I was sure the gun was not left from the World War II base but had been left in the cabin not so long ago by someone who planned to come back, or for emergency use by people who were shipwrecked or somehow stranded there.

I decided then that I needed to carry it around to protect myself against cougars and bears. We hadn't seen any, but that didn't matter.

These days people frequently see wolves up on the beaches nearby, but we never saw any tracks in 1971. Leaving the gun behind, I went up to the light station to see if Graham was free. He was home and welcomed me into the house.

He had just received a copy of *John Lennon/Plastic Ono Band*, John Lennon's first solo album, had only played it once, and was eager to play it for me. So we sat there for nearly an hour drinking coffee and listening to both sides of the album. It was moving to hear the lyrics to "Mother" for the first time, and a little shocking to listen to the blunt ode "Working Class Hero."

Pretty soon I figured I must have overstayed my welcome a little bit, and left Graham and headed back to the cabin at Guise Bay. I spent the rest of the day packing that rifle around, exploring the shoreline of Guise Bay, but except for some fishing debris from Japan, I suppose, there wasn't much of any interest there.

When I was growing up in Port Hardy, many people had collections of glass balls from Japan, where they were used as fishing floats for nets. We never found any when I was commercial-fishing with my father in the early 1960s off northern Vancouver Island, and I never found one on any beach trip either.

Carrying that Lee-Enfield around while I explored, I pondered whether I should keep it or not. I already had a .303 rifle at home and had in fact shot my first deer with it just the previous October. I didn't really need another hunting rifle, so in the end I decided to leave the rifle where I found it.

What became of it, I will never know. It was probably taken by someone after all, but it is not on my conscience.

I spent one more night on the squeaky bedsprings, and the next day I hiked all the way out, pausing to admire the Spencer house once again before continuing, still grateful for that first warm, dry night on the trail. Sadly, that was the last I ever saw of the house. It was burned down later that year by a mentally ill person who'd been

The Spencer house was the last remaining building from the original Cape Scott settlement. It was burned shortly after I took this photo. *Michel Drouin photo*

sprung from a mental hospital by a friend and brought to Hansen Lagoon for a "nature" cure. Evidently, he had decided that the house was "evil" and had to be destroyed, so that was the end of the last remaining whole structure of the Cape Scott settlement.

After that, it was another muddy slog to the trailhead, and seeing as it was a work week, I was able to catch a ride with a guy in a company truck to Holberg and hitch home to Port Hardy.

I did not go back to Cape Scott for another four years, and then, in 1975, I ended up going there three times: once with my wife, Juliane, then with her and a friend visiting from California, and then finally in August with Juliane and her fifty-eight-year-old mother.

Back in Port Hardy after my hike, I returned to the house I was living in with my girlfriend, Pam. I'd moved out of my parents' place and was living with Pam at a house she rented off Nick Nicholson across the bay, near the O'Connor log dump where my dad worked and I occasionally helped him on weekends.

I was just about finished grade twelve and she was working

as a waitress at the Seagate Hotel, saving money to go to Europe.

We both knew quite a lot of people from our combined sets of friends, and with the Island Copper Mine under construction and about to start production, Port Hardy was suddenly flooded with a whole bunch of newcomers, some of whom became friends as well.

What happened next at our happy little home surprised us both.

17 / **Keg Party**

AT THE THIRD STRIKE of the screwdriver, the beer spurted out of the hole in the top of the keg like a fountain, with a loud *pshhhh*. It hit the ceiling and rained down on everyone at the party, prompting a scramble into the kitchen cupboard for pots and pans and any other kind of container to capture the precious, foaming treasure.

Pam and I were renting the Nicholsons' house on the other side of the bay when either we decided to have a party, or a party decided to happen at our place. Probably the latter. We weren't party animals at all.

It was really Pam who was renting the place. She was the only one with a job. I can't remember the exact circumstances, but at one point we even had a social worker and two boys from the Tsulquate Reserve staying with us. I can't remember if that was a formal fostering arrangement or just that there was no other place to put them. It helped with the rent, though. Pam wasn't making much money to speak of in her low-paying service industry jobs. Or maybe she was bartending by then. I was too young to go to the bar, ironically enough, but she was older than me.

The social worker and the boys were not there anymore, and we were having a party at the house, which was tucked away at the end of a short driveway almost at the very end of the logging road to the O'Connor Logging log dump.

It was quiet over there, and hardly anyone ever came out that way except for one or two people who lived a little farther along the road and up a short track behind the log dump.

And this party started going. At first, people brought cases of beer and maybe a bottle of vodka or two as well, I can't remember, but eventually all the booze ran out, and as there was now a houseful of people, everyone was still thirsty.

Then someone had a bright idea.

"Hey, you know the beer parlour in Port McNeill gets its beer delivered down to the government dock and they can't store it all at the Dalewood, so there are kegs in the warehouse at the end of the dock," someone said.

So somebody volunteered to drive over to Port McNeill, which was about a forty-minute drive from Port Hardy, and have a look. Somehow or the other I ended up on the crew too. He only had a pickup truck, so it was just three of us.

What I remember is driving down to the government dock in Port McNeill. It was quite dark all around; I doubt if they even had any kind of street lighting down there at the time.

First, we looked at the big, corrugated-steel sliding barn doors of the building and noticed that they were securely padlocked shut, of course.

The driver turned the truck around and backed up to the door and got out. He rummaged around in the back of his truck and found a length of chain and attached it to the big steel handle of the warehouse door, left a little slack, then attached the other end to the bumper of his truck. When I and his other accomplice stood aside, he goosed the truck and it lurched forward, coming to a dead stop when it came to end of the chain. He spun his tires briefly, then backed up to give the chain full slack and accelerated again, breaking the padlock hasp right off and yanking the door open with a hell of a *clang*. I thought all of Port McNeill would have woken up hearing that.

We quickly ran in, and I don't remember if anyone had a flashlight or not, but we spotted the stacks of kegs, grabbed one and rolled it to the back of the truck, and with all three of us heaving we lifted the heavy canister into the pickup bed, slammed the tailgate shut and got the hell out of there.

Back at the house, the party was still going, and even more people had shown up, but they were dehydrated by the time we arrived. There was a shocked silence and then a big cheer when we rolled the keg in.

We propped it up on the kitchen table, but then a significant problem became apparent.

We had a keg full of beer, but we didn't know how to get the beer out of the keg.

Everybody was standing around, thirsty for the beer that was in the keg, and no one knew how to get it out. Finally, one of the guys went out to his vehicle and came back with a big screwdriver and a hammer. He picked the spot where the keg tap was supposed to go and started hammering away on the back end of the screwdriver, trying to get the cap off.

As soon as the tip of the screwdriver penetrated the edge of the tap bung on the keg, the beer spouted out. Every receptacle in the house, right down to a floor bucket, was utilized to try to salvage some of the beer.

Of course, it was all foam at first, and it seemed to take ages for the head to settle down and make some beer available to drink.

The house stank of beer for weeks afterward. It's a good thing the owner didn't drop by to have a look.

The Nicholson house wasn't the first house we'd lived in together. When I first started seeing Pam, she was living in a different place, a floathouse at the head of the bay, right in the estuary. It was the fall of 1970, and before I moved in permanently with Pam, I would stay at my parents' house during the week when I was going to school, and stay with her on the floathouse over the weekend.

We were still in bed one Saturday morning in early November when there was a tentative *tap-tap-tap* on the door, so I got up to answer it.

It was my dad, standing there and shuffling from one foot to the other, not quite looking me in the eye and avoiding looking in the house. "Michel, can you come and help me? I've got some deer down up in the meadow," he said, referring to his favourite hunting spot off the Holberg road.

"Some?" I asked. My dad was forty-five years old at the time and in very good physical condition. Why couldn't he carry the deer out himself?

"Well, there's three," he admitted. "I can't drag them out by myself."

So I got him to drive me home to get some decent boots and clothes for the effort, and we went up to the meadow, well off the road. Two of the deer were small bucks, and we were each able to drape one across our shoulders and pack it out, but it took both of us, one on each antler, to drag out the bigger third buck.

By staying overnight with Pam, I'd missed out on the best hunting day in my dad's life, but I'd already got my first deer just the month before and didn't feel like I had to hunt anymore that season.

18 / Deer Hunting

I HAVE BEEN DEER HUNTING almost as long as I can remember.

My father didn't take me along at first, but as soon as I was old enough to walk in the bush or ride in the truck with him, I did go along.

My dad liked hunting up near a lake about nine and a half miles to the west of Port Hardy, called Kains Lake. There was a foot trail to the lake before the logging road was built west, where it eventually met up with the maze of logging roads punched in from Holberg on the other side of the island.

There was a log cabin at Kains Lake belonging to an Italian-born man in Port Hardy called Joe Kilby. Joe Kilby always seemed old to me. He cut a lot of people's hair. I even went to him a few times when I was a teenager, before I quit getting haircuts altogether. I always thought that the cabin was just built there on Crown land, or that maybe he had a trapping or mining lease permitting the cabin, but I only found out in 2020 that he owned a large chunk of property there. I don't know who owned it between the time he died and time it changed hands in the twenty-first century.

From the first time I remember my father bringing a deer home, I wanted to do that too.
Rita Drouin photo

Joe Kilby had bought the cabin and land from a man called Thomlinson, who had homesteaded it under the pre-emption laws in place in the early part of the century. A trail had been surveyed into the Kains Lake area in 1913 from the trail to Coal Harbour and was completed when the Coal Harbour trail was cleared in 1916. Numerous settlers attempted farming in the rough and boggy area around Kains Lake, but when the promised road to Port Hardy never appeared, and the extremely tough homesteading conditions never improved, most gave up by 1920.

The Thomlinson homestead was next to one settled by a man called Jenkinson. There was a dispute between Jenkinson and Thomlinson about exactly where the property boundary was, and they were rumoured to have taken potshots at each other. The two men avoided each other to the point that instead of using the same walking trail from Port Hardy as Jenkinson, Thomlinson took a more roundabout route. He would load his supplies in a skiff and row north out of Hardy Bay, go west along the shore of Vancouver Island and come ashore at the mouth of Songhees Creek. There he would hide his boat on the shore and pack his supplies inland to Georgie Lake, where he had a raft that he used to cross the lake before packing his supplies south to his homestead at Kains Lake.

My dad knew where Jenkinson's cabin was hidden in the bush about a mile or two short of Joe Kilby's cabin. In the mid-1950s, when we still had a cocker spaniel named Skipper, my dad and his friend Joe Ackerman hiked the footpath up to the hidden cabin to go deer hunting. The cabin, though it had been abandoned for many years, was still solidly intact, with a functioning wood stove. Various people from Port Hardy had visited over the years since it had been abandoned in the 1930s, but it was still in fine shape. I never knew who told my father about it or provided instructions on how to get there. He knew that Skipper followed him wherever he went, so he told my mother to keep the dog inside until they were long gone.

I may have heard this story shortly after it happened when I was two or three, but I remember it clearly, probably from the numerous retellings I heard over the years.

After a long day of hiking up the trail, they got to the cabin, and my dad was in front of the cabin with an axe, chopping wood, when suddenly there was a blur of brown in the middle of the meadow where the trail emerged from the forest and Skipper ran into view, having followed their scent nine miles up the trail. Bounding behind Skipper was a cougar, who in one more leap was on top of the dog and had his head in its mouth. My dad yelled to Joe, who had his rifle handy, and before the cougar could do any more damage, he shot the cougar and it dropped, releasing the dog as it did.

I didn't get up to that cabin to go hunting until years later, when the logging road went in nearly parallel to the old trail, as it turned out. I guess that might have been around 1963 or '64. My dad drove up to what he used to call "8-Mile" because of the mile marker by the side of the road, parked and then walked into the forest and along to the river. It must have taken a few tries to get oriented, but after the first couple of times he had it figured out and knew exactly where to go to get to the log bridge and the Jenkinson cabin.

Jenkinson must have been one of the last holdouts of the original settlers in the area. He had built a very nice cabin at the edge of one of the larger natural meadows that exist up there in the middle of the island. The first few times I went in there with my father, the whole place was still intact. I don't know if anyone else had even been to the cabin since he had been about ten years before. There was still some canned food on the shelves, and I found a tide book from 1928 there.

The original survey crew must have fallen that huge log that acted as a bridge, unless it was the settlers. It had been a huge tree growing by the edge of the small river gorge and it had been cut so that it crossed the river. When I first saw it, it had the remains of split-cedar slabs that had been nailed to the surface as a footpath and even the remains of a handrail, but they were too shaky to use. We used that bridge quite a few times, despite the dizzying effect of the rushing water underneath that could disorient you.

Right near the bridge on the other side was a log cougar trap. It was a small rectangular log structure with a solid log top and slots in the front where a thick plank made of split wood was meant to slide. I suppose the sliding trap door was designed to slip shut when an animal entered and took a bait, triggering the door. It was crumbing into the ground and moss-covered when I first saw it, and no one knew if it had ever worked as a cougar trap.

The cabin, though, reached after a short twenty-minute walk into the forest, was remarkably well preserved.

It was finely built of logs, with a door and a window in front and another window on the side. It had a high peaked roof made of long split-cedar shingles, but unlike the shakes most people use

My father and me in front of the remains of the Jenkinson cabin. The roof caved in after a heavy snowfall in 1969. *Author's collection*

for roofing, these were about four or five feet long. The steep gable helped to shed the heavy snow that still fell there abundantly in the 1960s.

Inside, through the well-made wooden door hanging on leather hinges made from old boots, the place was clean and dry. I don't even remember much evidence of rodent activity.

I remember going there numerous times with my father, even after I got my first rifle and started hunting with him. He had gone back with David O'Connor one time, and I believe they may even have stayed the night. I sure wish I had, but sad to say that was something I never did.

In the spring of 1966, I was down at Fisherman's Wharf, trying to flog off my few extra *Vancouver Sun* newspapers from my paper route for cash to boat dwellers and itinerant boaters when I ran into our ex-neighbour Bill Scotton, whose house I used to visit when I was five and six years old.

When I ran into Bill in the spring of 1966, he was in his cabin cruiser. By then, Bill lived in Mexico in the winter and on the boat in the summer, working as a fisheries guardian for the Department of Fisheries and Oceans. He was headed north to watch creeks, which was primarily what contract fisheries guardians did in those days, to keep marauding commercial fishermen from "creek-robbing" by netting salmon at the mouths of small streams when they returned to spawn.

So I sold him a *Vancouver Sun* newspaper and we started talking about this and that, and he was telling me about Mexico. That was the first time I ever heard the word *mordida*, or "bite," which was what you called a bribe that you paid to policemen to ignore a traffic violation or to just plain leave you alone when they stopped you to put the bite on you.

He talked a little bit about smuggling a shotgun into Mexico and duck hunting down there somewhere. The talk turned to deer hunting and suddenly he asked, "Do you have a rifle?"

I admitted that I did not have one. I didn't have the money to buy one either, or rather, I had spent what money I did have from my paper route on a ten-speed bicycle the year before. Seeing as you could get an army-surplus, cut-down, sporterized .303 Lee-Enfield rifle from the Simpsons-Sears catalogue for $34.95 at the time, I suppose I might have been considering that, but I had to answer "No, I don't" to the question.

That was when he offered me one.

"You know that floathouse up in the bay there next to Bob Murray's?" Bill asked me.

I said yes, I did, I sold the odd extra newspaper to the older single guys who lived there. They were mostly alcoholics in between part-time jobs.

"Well, that's my floathouse," Bill explained. "I'm renting it to those guys. There's a rifle hanging up on nails between the kitchen and bedrooms. You can have that one if you want."

I knew the gun well. I had even gone into the house when nobody was home and taken it down and admired it. It was a .303—for some reason, I just knew that—but unlike any other .303 I had ever seen, it was a Ross rifle. Ross was a Canadian manufacturer that supplied rifles to the Canadian army in World War I. This rifle had an unusual action in that it was a bolt-action, but unlike the Lee-Enfield, where you had to turn the bolt up to pull it back and shove it forward and fold the bolt down to cock and shoot the gun, all you had to do was pull the bolt back and shove it forward to lock it.

I'd seen that in action one time, when Mike LeCerf, one of the floathouse dwellers, was blind drunk and in some kind of delirium. He saw my friend Kevin and me on the beach outside the house and came out onto the landing brandishing the rifle, cocked it and pointed it at us, raving that "I'm going to kill all you fuckers!" Fortunately, it wasn't loaded.

"Oh yeah, I've seen that rifle," I said.

"Well, you can go and take it down from there and have it," Bill said.

Boy, this was so exciting I could barely contain myself. I wanted to rush off right away and get it, but I had to stay and politely continue the visit and gab with Bill for at least a little while before going to the house and going in and grabbing the rifle.

I'd been in a spot of bother with the law before Christmas, so I didn't want to be seen walking down the road past Fisherman's Wharf with a rifle, so I stuck to the beach, walking around Bob Murray's floathouse, under Fisherman's Wharf and all the way along the shore past the remaining houses, to the Glen Lyon River bridge. I managed to hop across the rocks at the mouth of the river and skirted along in front of the three other houses on the shore until I got home.

For some reason, I already knew a little bit about Ross rifles. I guess it was because I was always interested in guns, and when the adults were talking about them my ears perked up and I listened with interest. There was no Internet then, of course, and even references in books were hard to come by. I remember hearing that the .280 Ross, a sporting calibre, had been a wonder cartridge for its time with amazing accuracy and killing power.

Apparently, there had been issues with the Ross rifle in World War I, and I had one of these examples, though mine had had the top stock wood removed, the fore-end shortened, the barrel cut back and the front sight remounted onto the shortened barrel. The problem with Ross rifles, as I understood it, was that the straight-pull bolt would sometimes drive backwards on the shot rather than remaining in the rifle, seriously injuring if not killing the shooter. So I had to make sure mine wouldn't do that.

On one weekend, I carried the rifle across the bay and, with my friend Bruce along, went up an old logging skid road until we came to an abandoned skidder tire. I secured the rifle inside the tire, pointed it safely into the trees, loaded it, and using a string attached to the trigger, fired it. It worked flawlessly. I tried it a few more times and nothing bad happened, so I was good to go.

I'd been in trouble the year before, and my parents thought it was better for me to leave Port Hardy for a while, so after I finished grade eight, I was sent to live with an aunt and uncle in Montreal and attend a Catholic school. I didn't get back to Port Hardy until August 1968, just before the start of hunting season. And now I had my own rifle too.

I went out with my dad to his usual haunts, but somehow that fall I just didn't connect with a deer. In addition to going into the woods and hunting around the Jenkinson cabin, my father had hidden a small rowboat in the bush at Kains Lake, and sometimes we would row over to the other side of the lake and hunt from Joe Kilby's cabin.

I got my first shot at a deer in the woods on the way to the Jenkinson cabin.

After crossing the river, my dad and my younger brother Marc were walking about forty yards ahead of me across a small meadow-like clearing in the forest when I caught a flash of movement over to my left, and a buck with a significant rack of antlers emerged from the trees. I stopped right there, flicked my safety off, aimed for a point right behind the front shoulder and pulled the trigger. *Boom!* went the old .303 Ross, and the deer dropped. Wow! I hadn't even had time to get excited, and shooting it had happened so swiftly, so I just stood there in awe at the deer on the ground. But it didn't stay there. In a second, it was up and running, dodging right in front of my dad, only about twenty yards in front of him. He shot and we saw fur fly, but the deer kept on going. *Shit!* My first deer and it hadn't stayed dead.

We could find no blood trail at all. I couldn't figure out what the heck had happened. I was certain I had aimed for its vitals. Maybe I hit it too far back, in the guts, which wouldn't be imme-diately fatal, but we didn't find any sign of stomach contents any-where on the ground either.

We searched and searched fruitlessly, went back to Port Hardy, and borrowed a couple dogs off Marvin Vestad: Brittany spaniels, but they were pretty much useless. We tried to show them the site of the dropped deer and let them loose, but all they did was run around in circles, excitedly barking. So, sad to say, my first deer got away from me.

I don't remember if I went hunting with my dad in 1969 or not. I spent the summer of 1969 in Sointula, playing in a band and clearing some land for Larry Sommer, but my memory is kind of blank for the fall of 1969.

It was in 1970 that I went hunting again with my dad at Kains Lake. Using the rowboat, we crossed the lake, landed slightly to the east of the cabin, and started out through the meadows. We split up, with me heading directly behind the Joe Kilby cabin and my dad angling over to the right, more in the direction of the Jenkinson cabin.

I always enjoyed hunting in the meadows on the other side of Kains Lake. For some reason, the trees never got very big, and the area was a combination of long, narrow meadows on flat ground with little forested ridges appearing occasionally. It was perfect hunting country. You'd walk along a meadow or, better yet, skirt around the edge of it, scrutinizing both sides of it as you crossed. Then there would be a low ridge of small trees and berry bushes you'd have to traverse, and from the top of the ridge you could look down into the next meadow without disturbing it or being seen.

The ground in the meadows was soft and spongy sometimes, with little sloughs running across it, draining water down toward the lake. A few were quite wide and a challenge to jump across. The fragrance in the air was something that I will never forget: a spicy sent of yellow cedar branches and dried grass, just a little bit like hay. The Labrador tea bushes growing in abundance there added their own scent to the potpourri of fragrances. I'd pick a few leaves of Labrador tea and chew on them or even stick them between my gums and teeth like Copenhagen snuff to savour the tangy flavour.

I was walking along this way; across the second meadow I had come to that morning, looking forward to coming to the next ridge because there were the remains of a cabin that someone had built on it many years before. There really wasn't much left of it, but on cold November days we could still find remnants of cedar shakes to start a fire with. It was still October, though, and not cold enough to warrant starting a fire.

I must have had a premonition or something, but I was really "on" that morning, so after crossing that last meadow, I gingerly made my way up the next small ridge, parting bushes and marsh willow aside so that I could carefully make my way through them. I reached the top, paused for a moment, and then just as gingerly descended into the next meadow. I was just at the bottom of the ridge where it met the level ground again, slightly screened by some low bushes, when I saw a flicker of movement forward and to my left about sixty or seventy yards away.

It was a doe, and right behind her was a buck. And not just any buck either; it had significant antlers perched on its head. I didn't hesitate. I didn't have time to hesitate. I just slipped the safety off my rifle, aimed for the middle of the buck's neck, and pulled the trigger. The buck dropped right there, and the doe bounded away. I stood there in awe of what had just happened, then hurriedly walked over to the prone animal. It was a happy/sad moment for me. I had finally shot my first deer, but I had taken a life, and as I stood there the eyes lost their vitality and spark.

Now that the initial excitement was over and the deer was lying still on the ground, I took another look at the head. It had the largest rack I'd ever seen on an island deer. Well, not very wide like mule deer I had seen photos of, but this buck had four points on each side, plus one extra on one side that stuck out like a dagger.

Now I had to field-dress it. I had first seen my dad gut a deer when I was eleven, six years before, and had been along on other trips when he had shot and dressed out a deer, so for some reason I didn't feel daunted by it at all. It was just part of the process, but seeing as it was the first time I had ever done it by myself, I was a little intimidated. But about forty minutes later I had the guts out and the heart and liver put aside, and started thinking of dragging the deer out.

Most of the time the deer my dad shot there in the meadows were small enough to sling across your back, with the front legs down one side of your chest and the back legs down the other, but there was no way this deer was going to be carried out by one man. I was grateful that when I was just finishing gutting the deer, my dad showed up, out of breath. "I've been looking all over for you," he said. "I was just lining up on one myself when you shot, but it got away. I knew you were over here somewhere, but I went over one meadow too many." He paused, looking down at my buck. "That's a dandy," he said.

Together we dragged the deer down to the lakeshore and my father walked along the shore to the rowboat and brought it to pick up the deer. We loaded the deer into the rowboat and made our way back across the lake to the short little gravel-topped landing that went from the Holberg road to the water's edge. We unloaded the deer and our gear and then rowed the skiff around a little point and put it in it its hiding spot.

After we dragged the deer up to the truck parked beside the road, and retrieved our rifles and things, I was resting on a log nearby and having a smoke when a couple guys stopped because they saw we had a deer. I still remember one of them; his name was Wayne Fox.

My dad started telling the story about hiking along and seeing a buck and just getting ready to shoot it and how it took off. Then Wayne said. "Well, if you didn't shoot this deer, who did?"

"Oh, my son there shot this one," my dad said. I still remember them looking at me, a scrawny seventeen-year-old with long hair and a thick beard, and I swear their jaws dropped.

After processing the deer at home, I couldn't figure out how to save the head and its antlers, so I tied it to a rope and dropped it to the bottom at the log boom, hoping the crabs would clean it up. They didn't, as it turned out, but at least it got to kind of rotting underwater. It stank when I brought it up to check, so I dropped it in again. Eventually, some of the flesh got eaten, but I had to pull it up before losing it, so I put it in the back yard. The flesh finally came off it and I had it around for years. It got brittle, though, and eventually split in half and I abandoned it at the cabin when we moved to Vancouver years later.

I kept hunting with that .303 Ross rifle until I got married in 1974, and when I told my wife Juliane about the gun's reputation for going off backwards, she got nervous and recommended I get another one to replace it. I borrowed a couple of rifles off my old grade-two schoolteacher, Mrs. Eckley, as her hunting husband Harold was deceased, but I found the .30-06 too heavy and likely too powerful for the little island deer I was hunting, and similarly the .308 I borrowed off her was very damaging to a deer I shot with it, so I returned them. Had I known that I was about to take up black bear hunting, and eventually elk and moose too, I might have kept that .308, but it wasn't the gun I wanted at the time.

I was on the lookout for a decent sporterized or even full-military-configuration 7x57 Mauser rifle, but there just weren't any in the places I looked, and I wasn't haunting Lever Arms in Vancouver at the time, as I didn't hardly ever go to Vancouver.

Then one day I was in a little corner store that one of the Shanks family started on Market Street in Port Hardy, and noticed that they had four rifles for sale: a Cooey .22 rifle, a Cooey single-shot 12-gauge shotgun, a Remington BDL in .222, and a Remington ADL in .243. The BDL was a higher-end rifle, with a hinged floor plate for easier unloading, and the ADL was a plain-Jane rifle, but the idea of the .243 calibre interested me, so I went to the bank and got the cash, and for $180 I was the proud owner of a Remington .243.

My cousin Richard had recently come to BC from Quebec, and I think we were headed to Port Alice in his van to attend the fall fair there. There wasn't much happening culturally on northern Vancouver Island at that time, so even a fall fair in the next town was something to look forward to. Before leaving I said, "Let's take my new rifle, I want to try it out." So, with the rifle still in its green Remington box and a new box of Imperial-brand ammunition I'd bought, we set out for Port Alice. Somewhere along the way we pulled off at a logging road and I set up a target on a stump, and using the iron sights I proceeded to take the first shots with my new rifle. It went off with a loud bang, but I was pleasantly surprised at the low recoil of the rifle. And I was even more pleased at the group. Right out of the box, without any adjusting of the sights, shooting at seventy-five yards, I had put three shots into a circle the size of a quarter, right where I had been aiming. That's what I was looking for. Now I could go hunting!

***

I started hunting with that rifle right away, during hunting season in September 1976, when Juliane was seven months pregnant. I was working at the time, so I was only able to hunt on weekends and I didn't get a deer before our daughter was born on November 10. I did however get a nice, big, black bear.

Now, some people would say that a .243 is not enough gun to hunt black bears with, and when I was still looking, the guy in the sporting goods shop in Port McNeill told me that he thought a .270 was the bare minimum that you should go bear hunting with. But I was happy with my .243, and when I did finally shoot that bear, which turned out to be the biggest bear I ever shot in fifty-two years of hunting, it was with the .243. The trick was that I was not shooting a body shot, aiming for the vital organs, but aiming for the neck. It worked on that bear, that's for sure. It dropped at the shot.

One time, I was hunting over there in the meadows, and I was in a particularly narrow one, walking along the very edge of it, when I heard a crunching noise over in the thicket to my left. I stopped and waited. Sometimes it went silent and there was a sound of bushes being shoved aside, a little crack of a branch, nothing, and then another snippet of sound. Not knowing what to expect, I slipped my safety off and waited. Suddenly, right in front of me, about thirty yards away, a buck walked into the narrow strip of meadow at a brisk pace. He appeared so quickly that I didn't even have a chance to raise my rifle. Suddenly, a doe appeared right behind him, walking almost on her elbows, following him closely, sniffing the ground behind him and *baa*-ing like a sheep. Must have been mating season. They both got safely across the meadow and into the bush before I could react.

I remember that a few years later my dad and I went out up to the lake, paddled across to the other side in a canoe and went hunting. We pretty much did the same routine we usually did when we were hunting over there: split up and go our own way, and then if the other guy shot something, we'd walk over toward the shot and often find each other.

I was sneaking from meadow to meadow as usual this time when I saw a brief movement of brown and saw it was the side of a deer. I guess it had spotted me first, but instead of running away, it just stood behind a tangle of low trees and berry bushes and looked back at me. I still had not mounted a scope on my rifle, and all I could see of this deer was its head face-on to me with the antlers poking up above the ears. Definitely a buck! So I slowly raised the rifle and aimed for the middle of the nose. I fired and it disappeared. *Shit*. I must have missed. I walked over for a look and there was the deer, a nice two-point with a bullet hole right in the middle of its nose.

***

There were lots of times when I was a kid that I did not go with my dad on hunting trips. They were always day trips, and one of my big regrets in life is that we never went and spent the night at the Jenkinson cabin, but oh well…

Starting at about the age of twelve, when my dad came home with a deer, I'd often help him hang it up, and then he'd ask me, or tell me, really, "You skin it, Michel." So I got pretty good at skinning deer.

I tried numerous times to save deer hides and tan them, but there was very little information available at the time. Port Hardy didn't have a library, really; there was a handful of books in a little corner room of the community hall, but nothing of any use. My parents didn't have an encyclopedia, and nobody seemed to know anything about how to do it. My father did say that alum was used to preserve hides, but that was pure unobtanium in a place with no pharmacy. The best thing to do was cover the thing with salt and try to dry it out that way, but the problem was that the climate was so damp that even if you found an area large enough to lay out a hide on a piece of plywood and cover it in salt, the salt absorbed more moisture out of the air than it drew out of the hide.

I never did manage to preserve a deer hide the whole time I was growing up.

Later, when I was a teenager, my skill with deer carcasses came into use to help other people. I was visiting my girlfriend Pam at the floathouse where she lived on the other side of the bay when these two Czech guys, who lived in a small cabin on the same float, came knocking at the door after dark.

I answered the door. There stood Dennis and Jan. Dennis's real name was Zedenek, but he preferred to be called Dennis. He was a waiter at the Seagate. Jan did labouring jobs.

"Michel, can you helping us?" Dennis asked. Ever the agreeable sort, I said sure, what did they need?

"We just shot a deer and don't have time to do anything with it before we go to court," they explained. They'd shot it by pit-lamping too, which means catching an animal at night, blinding it with a bright light and shooting it, a serious wildlife-law offence—and now here they had to rush off to a court date for some other issue. We still had a citizen magistrate's court in those days, and court was often held in the evening.

"Okay, sure, where is it?" I asked, and they took me outside onto the float and down the walkway to the door of a shed near their little cabin. There was the dead deer. Not only had they shot a deer illegally by pit-lamping, but they had shot a doe, also illegal, and in the guts, which was not only stupid but gross too. Oh god, what had I agreed to?

I didn't have a hunting knife with me while visiting with Pam at the floathouse, so I went into the house and found a couple of knives that might be up to the task. Taking a flashlight with me, I went out to deal with this pathetic little deer they'd shot. I don't know how many shots those idiots had taken at this deer, but they had sure figured out how to mess it up.

So somehow I got the inside of the deer cleaned up as best as I could, and I might have got some water and tried to douche it out with water and rags. Then I had to hang it up, which wasn't easy by myself—I might have got Pam to help. And then I skinned it for them too.

I don't recall if those guys ever even said thank you.

It was around this time that I started working weekends with my dad on the log booms.

19 / **Booming Logs**

I **WENT TO WORK FULL-TIME** on the log booms in Port Hardy with my father, right out of high school. After working the odd weekend, I kind of knew the routine a bit already.

My dad often had a Gwa'sala man named Henry George working with him, but Henry was also a fisherman, so in the summer he would quit to go fishing. That was how I got a full-time job on the boom working for O'Connor Logging in Port Hardy in June 1971.

First, I had to get a pair of caulk boots. For some reason loggers always called them "cork" boots. I still don't know why. One interpretation I read stated that some English people pronounced *caulk* as "cork," and this pronunciation spread throughout the industry. And they were expensive. It was the equivalent of two days' pay to buy a pair of caulk boots. So off I went to the commissary at the M&B logging camp run by Robert Scott, owner of the hardware store in town. The commissary was only open certain hours, so I had to make sure I got there at the right time.

I don't know if Scott stocked both Dayton and Pierre Paris boots there, or if all he had was Pierre Paris boots, but I ended up buying a pair of Pierre Paris & Sons caulks there, plus a can of Protex boot

I could hardly wait until I was big enough to wear my own pair of caulk boots. *Rita Drouin photo*

grease. Pierre Paris & Sons was a competitor to Dayton Boots at the time, and loggers had their preferences. Either way, when a pair of boots cost $80 and you were only going to be making $3.90 an hour, that was a major expense.

MacMillan and Bloedel still had their booming ground in operation on the south side of the bay, right in front of the estuary of the Quatse River. When my father had first signed on there in 1953, they were still making flat booms and had a huge crew, as they were hand-stowing every boom and it took a lot of people to do that.

All wood was being shipped out in bundle booms now, meaning that the logging-truck loads of logs were not dumped loose into the water, but had cables around them to keep them intact so that instead of great numbers of flat booms, each boom was made up of bundles of logs, making the shipping of them to town much more efficient.

One complication, though, was that the logs had to be sorted to a degree before they were put on trucks, so that saw logs—that is, logs destined for the sawmill—were separated from pulp, and big spruce logs or "peelers" were kept separate because they would go to a plywood mill. Red cedar was kept separate from other logs as well.

The M&B operation on the south side of the bay was still pretty large compared with the O'Connor Logging booming ground on the north side of the bay, where my dad worked. The O'Connor booming ground only had two stowing pockets, so when he was booming up more than two types of wood, the other bundles had to drift around loose in the bullpen, where they were first dumped from trucks.

Seeing as there were frequently three or four sorts of wood being dumped into the water at the same time—small, medium and large saw logs, for example, as well as pulp bundles—he had to work fast getting the booms built and out of there in order to keep the wood flowing from the logging operations.

My father was making five-section booms for O'Connor. The bundles of logs were lined up inside a frame of broomsticks five long and one across.

I had already learned up at the Nahwitti River and at this booming ground on weekends what making up a set of "sticks" consisted of. The company would send down a bundle of logs destined to be boomsticks, all consistently sixty-six feet long, not too tapered, big enough at the top end to withstand being chained together and pulled along, and not too large in the butt, so that we could drill holes in them.

There was a particular order in which you had line up the logs after you had drilled them, so that when they were chained together and then placed in the pocket for stowing, all five side sticks were facing top forward. They had to be arranged in the correct order in the boomstick pen so that when you chained them up top-to-butt except for the head and tail sticks, grabbed them and pushed them out of the pen into the water with the dozer boat and unfolded them, they folded out perfectly in line, ready to be put into the stowing pocket.

My father worked through most of the 1950s at the booming ground of Alice Lake Logging (a subsidiary of the Powell River Company). The company merged with MacMillan and Bloedel in 1960. *Marcel Drouin photo*

As soon as I started on the boom with my dad, he got me drilling holes in logs for sets of boomsticks while he stowed some bundles. There was other work to do once the logs were stowed, but he could do that by himself with the boat while I drilled the "sticks."

The first thing we had to do to make up a set of boomsticks was to break the bundle open. When the bundles were dumped from the trucks, they had two cables tied around them, each one about one quarter of the way from the end. We had to climb on top of the bundle with a "guillotine," which was a heavy, flat-bottomed cutter that we placed on a log, slide the cable into it, then, with a sledgehammer, whack the top of the cutter, which was a hardened steel or tungsten blade inside the cylindrical shaft of the unit. It might take two or three tries before the cable was cut through, and then you had to grab the guillotine before it fell off the log and into the water as the bundle started to separate at that end. But then you still had to cut the second cable. That procedure was the same only trickier, because on the final whack on the cutter with an eight-pound sledgehammer, the cable separated, the logs started to roll, and you had to grab the cutter by the rope loop attached to it with your one free hand, then run down the rolling logs to the stable stiff-leg next to the boring machine.

The boring machine was an old single-cylinder diesel engine that was started with a hand crank. It didn't have a spark plug or glow plug or anything like that; it had a little ignition plug that you had to insert into the top of the cylinder every time you wanted to start the engine. There was a little shaft with a handle that you had to unscrew out of the top of the motor that had a little cylindrical hole in the end. We had cans of these little ignition plugs on hand. They were about the length of half a cigarette and had ignition material on the end, so that they had a red tip. We had to fit the plug into the end of the little shaft so that the red end was visible, then screw it back into the top of the motor. After setting the throttle and making sure the machine was out of gear—or we couldn't turn the handle at all—we had to hand-crank the starting handle around and around until we were turning the motor fast enough to start it with our right hand, then turn a little lever on the engine with our left hand, and hopefully the built-up compression would fire the single spark plug to get the motor going. The whole procedure was a lot like starting an old gasoline-powered Easthope engine.

That little motor was very loud for what it was, with each ignition of the cylinder sounding like a 20-gauge shotgun blast, and we had to wear ear protection, inadequate as it was in those days.

Sometimes we made up sticks together, if there was no other work like stowing to be done, but after the bundle of sticks was broken open, I was on my own drilling the holes in the ends of the logs.

First, I had to manoeuvre the log so that it would feed smoothly under the auger. Hopefully, the guys in the woods had paid attention to our requirements and had not sent down boomsticks with huge butts. A boomstick that was too large across the butt posed two problems. The first thing was that it wouldn't fit under the platform where we stood to run the boring machine; and the other problem was that when it came time to chain it up to another log, the chains might not reach from log to log.

We had a very short pike pole about four feet long to exactly adjust the end of the log before we dropped the auger onto it. To run the machine and bore the holes in the log, the motor had to be running, of course, then the log had to be manoeuvred into position under the four-inch auger. Standing on a solid-steel platform over the water and the log, we then had to engage the clutch to get the auger going and, using a big steel wheel, lower the moving auger onto the log. If we tried to drop the auger onto the log without engaging the motor, the auger would likely jam in the hole as it took the first few bites into the log.

If ear protection was inadequate on the boring machine, protection from the moving auger was even worse. Standing on the platform, using the short pike pole to wiggle the log exactly into place, then using the other hand to lower the moving auger onto the log, we had to stand barely twelve inches away from the moving auger.

We had our pants cut off short at the top of our boots to keep them from getting wet if we had to stand on sinking logs, and the sleeves of our jackets were similarly cut short, but still there was the danger of getting a piece of clothing caught in the auger if there was even a loose thread. It is amazing nobody got killed using those machines. Or at least I never heard of it happening.

I didn't think about it at the time, as we never had an incident, but thinking back on it now, working with no guard around that moving auger connected to the small but powerful engine could have easily resulted in catastrophic and probably fatal injuries.

If a pant leg had caught in the auger, it would have dragged the operator into it, breaking his leg immediately and wrapping his whole body around, bashing it into the rest of the drilling mechanism, around and around until there was nothing but mincemeat left. And nobody would know the difference unless the boat operator looked over and noticed nobody upright running the boring machine.

Good thing I didn't think about that at the time.

Once the auger was turning and drilling into the correct spot in the log, we usually didn't have to keep hold of the short pike pole and jammed it point-down nearby so that it would be easy to grab if needed. But now you had to really be careful drilling the hole. Chips would start to emerge out of the hole, and even if the auger was biting in well and drilling well, it had to be extracted using the big steel wheel to clear the hole before again lowering the giant drill bit into the log.

The fragrance of fresh wood wafted up from the hole, the smell varying with the type of wood. Spruce had the sweetest scent, but even hemlock or balsam was pleasant to the nose, a small respite from the noise and stink of the exhaust of the noisy little diesel engine.

If I kept clearing the hole, eventually I would penetrate the whole log and suddenly the drill bit would plunge right through, and I could hear the motor pick up revs, as it wasn't encountering any more resistance of the bit digging into the wood.

If the auger got stuck in the hole, though, oh boy, then you were in for some grief! First thing, the auger had to be disconnected from the driveshaft hanging down from the gearbox by undoing the four thick bolts that held it in place. Then the auger had to be unwound out of the hole with pipe wrenches, one difficult, slow turn at a time. Fortunately, that didn't happen too often, because we were pretty careful about frequently clearing the auger holes.

Once a hole was drilled into one end of the log, it had to be fed under the auger until the other end was positioned there and the procedure was repeated.

Once all twelve logs that were to make up the set of boom-sticks were drilled, they had to be arranged in the stick pocket in the correct order to be chained together to make one string.

Seeing as they had been stacked in the truck and bundled with all the tops facing the same way, after each stick was drilled, every second one had to be turned around inside the stick pocket so that it would link up correctly with the previous one. Except for the first two logs, which had to face the same direction, and two in the middle that had to have their tops facing the same direction, the top-to-butt-to-top-to-butt arrangement had to be continued.

Once the logs were all drilled and lined up in the correct order, it was time to connect them together with boom chains. The boom chains were seven feet long and weighed forty pounds or more, with a ring on one end that couldn't be pulled through the log, and a toggle on the other end. The way we connected the logs together with the boom chains was to drop a boom chain toggle down through the hole in the butt·of one log and then drop a "toggle hook" on a stout string down the hole in the top of the next log over and hook them together. First, we had to pull up the toggle hanging down from the chain with a pike pole, then fix the toggle hook to the toggle, put a half-hitch around the toggle, secure it tightly, then carefully drop it into the water, hoping it wouldn't undo. Then, keeping tension on the string with the toggle on the end, we had to draw it up through the hole in the log we had dropped the toggle hook through. If everything worked well, the toggle came smoothly up and then we laid it crossways across the hole. This procedure was repeated until the whole set had been chained together. Then each toggle was secured in place with a wooden plug we'd made up from small cedar blocks, sharpened on two corners and driven into the hole to keep the toggle in place.

If the boomsticks ever got connected incorrectly, which I confess I was guilty of once, when my father went to pull the string of logs out and they were supposed to unfold like a necklace, there would be two stuck together in the middle of the arrangement. What a mess!

Then he had to fold the whole works of them back up again and shove the set of sticks back into the boomstick pocket, and we had to disconnect the wrongly chained-up logs and do it all over again the right way. Even disconnecting the logs wasn't easy, because we had to extract the cedar plugs we had so diligently hammered into the hole with the toggle to keep it securely in there. But a judicious use of the pointed end of a peavey did the trick.

If the set of sticks had been correctly hooked up, it was easy to push them out of the pocket, hook the tow hook onto the ring of the outside one, and pull it out until it unfolded in a single line of twelve logs. Once out into the bay, in front of the empty stowing pocket we wanted to put it into, we'd tow it into the pocket and secure the sides with cables attached to the standing boom, which was made up of logs permanently anchored in place as a framework, and then the boomsticks were laid out and ready to be filled with bundles.

The bundles would be shoved in by dozer boat and usually stowed four or five wide. Because not all the logs in the bundles were of the same length, it was a trick like putting a puzzle together: once the first tier of logs was in place, you had to find a bundle to match it end to end so that the projecting logs fit into the next bundle and the tiers were evenly spaced across the boom.

Once the whole five-section boom was full of bundles, we closed off the end with the "tail stick," and then we had to put swifters across.

When my dad was working on the boom at Nahwitti, we used wire swifters, with dogs strung along them like beads on a necklace, and hammered them into the logs every section to keep them from slipping out of the boom once it was being towed. When they made flat booms in most booming grounds at the time, they pulled logs across every section, attaching them to the rings on the boom chains connecting each section together.

Here at O'Connor's booming ground in Port Hardy, we pulled logs across the bundles and attached them to the chains at each section's intersection with more chains. I say pulled, but it was a combination of pushing and pulling. My dad would take a boom-stick and, using the dozer boat, push the top of it up onto the standing boom, then go around to the back end of it, straighten it out so that it was in line with the opposite side of the boom, and shove it up as far as he could with the bow of the powerful little boat.

To help pull the swifter logs across the bundles, we had a boom winch on floats that operated from the side of the boom opposite the one where my dad was shoving the logs up. It was a rough covered shack over an ancient 1940s six-cylinder Dodge gas engine mounted on a wooden skid anchored to the float logs.

The engine was tricky to start. I had to stand on one of the skids, set the throttle where I wanted it to be when the engine started, and hold my hand palm down on top of the carburetor. The engine had no choke, so this was how we choked it. I then turned the key, and if the battery had any juice in it, the engine would turn over and the carburetor would start to try to suck air in. I would let it suck at the palm of my hand, then lift my palm just a little bit to let enough air in, and if I did everything right, the engine would roar into action. If I did it wrong, then I flooded the carb with gas and had to wait a few minutes to let the gas evaporate before I could try starting the engine again.

To pull a swifter log all the way across a boom, I had to disengage the lock on the drum loaded with cable so that it could freewheel, and then pull the cable out as far as it could reach. It wasn't long enough, so we had an extension that I had to add on to reach the tip of the log that my dad had pushed up on the other side.

After I pulled all the cable out and choked the end of the log, I returned to the machine and winched in the cable until the slack was all picked up, and then I pulled on it so that it got "singing tight," as my dad used to say. When he noticed that I had the slack picked up on my end, he took the bow of the dozer boat up against the butt of the log, revved up the boat and pushed full bore as I did the same with the winch, and together we pushed and pulled the log up onto the bundles. As long as we kept up the motion, most of the time the log would come smoothly across all four bundles and I could pull the end right above the other chains where we wanted to hook it up.

Once the log was in the correct location, we usually had enough slack to hook up the butt end to the ring at the junction of the boomsticks, but sometimes at the top end we had to use the winch to pull the top down low enough to connect it to the ring in the boomstick. It often took an extra boom chain to do that.

If things went well, the log came snaking smoothly across the ends of the bundles until it was nestled right where we wanted to connect it, which wasn't always the case. Sometimes the top end of the log I was pulling across plunged down and rammed up against a bundle so that I had to stop the winch, slack the cable, and go across the boom to see if there was some way I could wrap the cable around another log to lift it out of the hole it had dug itself into.

Sometimes, if there was a little hang-up, all I had to do was rev up the old Dodge and the tip of the log would pop up and I could keep pulling it in.

One time, though, when I was pulling a swifter log across a boom, it hung up, even though my father was pushing the butt with the dozer boat on the other end. I revved the engine and pulled harder. Still no go, so I revved up the engine even more, and SNAP!— before I even realized it, the extension cable I had on the end of the regular cable broke as the log sprang toward me without my even seeing it, and coiled itself at my feet. I still remember how, before I even realized what was happening, this perfect coil of cable wound itself onto the float right in front of where I was standing.

If the end of the cable had recoiled straight back at me, it could have taken an eye or both eyes out or cut my throat. I climbed up onto the bundle to signal to my dad that we had better stop and figure out how to pull that swifter log across without the extension.

***

That boom winch raft attracted otters. We rarely saw them, but when we got to work in the mornings there was often fresh otter shit on the logs. Now, the only thing worse than the smell of fresh otter shit is the stench of several days or even weeks of accumulated otter shit. When we didn't work Saturdays and had the whole weekend off and came back to work on Monday morning and there was two or three days' worth of otter droppings on the float, the old fish-stink was nearly incredible. I had an old five-gallon oil bucket on hand, and I'd fill it with sea water to wash most of the shit off the logs.

One morning there was a fresh nine- or ten-pound spring salmon sitting in between the logs of the float. It must have jumped out of the water right onto the raft. That was kind of amazing, because I don't remember ever seeing one jump in the bay and I used to spend a lot of time in the bay trolling for coho salmon when I was younger.

There were always mink along the shore near the booming ground, and we frequently saw them running on the logs. Some years later, after I was freshly married and working with my dad on the boom again, I found a newly deceased one floating in the water. I picked it up and brought it home to my new wife and presented it to her.

"Every woman wants a mink," I told her. "Here's yours."

My dad and I went out to the boom one cold morning when there was a thin skiff of fresh snow on the logs, and when we got over to the other side of the bay to go to work there was a deer on one of the bundles. I could understand why it was there. A fellow living in a house near our log dump had those yappy Brittany spaniels we'd borrowed when looking for the lost deer; they most likely had chased the deer into the water. Either that or wolves did, but wolves, though they did exist there, were not commonly seen near town. But what was really surprising was that the deer had actually been able to pull itself out of the water and onto the logs. It was standing on a bundle on a boom that we still hadn't finished making up, so we left it alone and went to work boring sticks or stowing into the next pocket over, and by lunchtime it was gone. I don't know where—it probably jumped into the water and swam back to shore, or was frightened by the dozer boat and jumped in and kept going to the other side of the bay.

The other side of the bay was where we tied up the log booms. Off at an angle to us, on a little point of land where there had been another log dump and booming ground in the early 1960s, was the Seafood Products cannery adjacent to the narrow entrance to the inner bay. The company had not yet built the extensive array of floats and mooring places that they soon would, so O'Connor Logging was able to use the water lot in front of the cannery to tie up the log booms whenever we completed enough for a full tow to town.

Once they were completed, we disconnected each five-section boom of logs and hooked up the tow line to the ring on the head stick and pulled it out of the stowing pocket and across the bay to the tie-up spot there in front of the cannery. Pilings had been driven into the bottom there, into groups that we called "dolphins," and we had cables hanging from these that we could attach the booms to. We arranged the first row of booms along the dolphins three booms long, and then as the next tier of booms was completed, we attached them to the first row with boom chains.

I remember one time we were starting the second tier of booms, and after we had towed the boom out into the bay, we unhooked the tow line and I disembarked onto the boom and walked across it. I had a boom chain already placed on the bundle at the first corner of the boom that was going to get connected, and my dad pushed on the outside of the boom to get the corner in place. Once they came together, I had to connect the chain from ring to ring as fast as possible because the motion and the pressure of the tons and tons of logs moving together would make the boom slide along the fixed one and the boomsticks could possibly climb up onto one another.

I had chained up the first corner of the boom, and my dad had moved over to the rear end of the boom with the dozer boat to shove it in so that I could chain up that end, and I started walking along the boomsticks to the opposite end, where I had to make the tie-up. I was about halfway along the last boomstick and the outside boom was rapidly coming closer and closer to the tied-up one, much like a door closing, when I stepped on a slippery piece of bark and before I knew it, I was up to my neck in the water as the booms were about to collide.

I didn't have time to think of the consequences, which would be dire. If I could not get out of the water, I would be crushed by the boomsticks closing up on me, either crushing the breath and life out of me or popping my head like a cantaloupe.

The alternative would have been to dive under the boom and hope to come up on the other side of the boomstick, within the boom itself, but the bundles were crammed in so tight that there was no space between them to surface in if I wanted to. Besides that, I was wearing a life jacket and I could not have submerged even if I had tried.

Suddenly, just as suddenly as I had fallen in, I was back up on the boomstick I had fallen off. I didn't have time to think about what had just happened. I proceeded to the end of the log where the two booms had now neatly met up corner to corner and ring to ring, and I joined the two together.

Then I had time to assess my clothing. I had been wearing rain pants with a bib and a rain jacket that was buttoned up almost all the way to the neck. I hadn't even really got wet, despite having been plunged into the water. Sure, my sleeves were wet from the ingress of water there, as was my neck and even the cuffs of my pants, but besides that, I was dry. I hadn't even got water in my boots.

By now my dad had run the dozer over to pick me up and we took off back to the booming ground. I didn't even tell him I'd fallen in until we went up for lunch at the shack at the log dump.

John the dump man was an interesting guy who had grown up in Bella Coola. He was a descendant of John Clayton, a Hudson's Bay Company employee who bought the company store and property in Bella Coola in 1882.

Almost every time we came in for coffee or lunch and had taken our seats, he'd sit back on his chair, grab hold of his suspenders with his thumbs, shove them out forward, stretching them about a foot off his chest, settle back and say, "Well, back on the ranch you know..." and he'd launch into a story about his days in Bella Coola and Chilcotin. He had lived there before the road was built to Williams Lake, so he had worked on horse-pack trains from the store in Bella Coola up to Anahim Lake, where his uncle had a ranch. He didn't mention it at the time, but I found out from his daughter many years later that he had owned a ranch there too.

***

The logs we were booming came from O'Connor's logging claims up off the Holberg road.

When I was young, there was no road to Holberg on the other side of the island, at the head of Holberg Inlet. In 1960 a road was started from Port Hardy that would eventually connect with logging roads from Holberg. Kains and Nahwitti lakes were beside the road, and a short way down a side road before Kains Lake, there was a third lake, called Georgie Lake.

I'd been told there was an A-frame cabin built by a Port Hardy family on the shore of the lake and I was determined to see it one day.

I eventually did do that, in the summer I turned thirteen, with my friend David. When we graduated from high school and I went to work on the boom, David went to work in the rigging. A few years later, when I had gone abroad for the third time and was living in Japan, he wrote me a letter saying he was getting married to a girl called Kimberly and would I please be his best man. I had to decline, as I had just moved in with a young German woman I had fallen in love with and wasn't ready to come home yet.

20 / David

THE SADDEST THING I EVER HAD TO DO while living in Port Hardy was bury my friend David's wife.

When I arrived back in Port Hardy in the fall of 1974 after setting up the immigration of my German girlfriend, Juliane, as a sponsored fiancée, I met Kimberly for the first time.

She was a tiny little woman, still a girl really; I don't know if she was even twenty years old. We were barely twenty-one ourselves.

David had been a close friend since we were kids in elementary school. He was living out at the reserve in Fort Rupert when we first started hanging around. I would ride my bike the seven miles of rough road to go play and hang out with him and some of the other kids I was friends with, like Ernie Jacobson and Buster Wilson and his brothers.

I used to like it out at the reserve. It had been kind of a forbidden place to us as white people, I thought, but they showed me things like the old Hudson's Bay store and the community smokehouse. The funny thing, though, is that they never showed me the petroglyphs down on the beach.

I felt accepted while hanging around in Fort Rupert too. In Port Hardy there was always some white kid, often older, who would make fun of me, saying that Michel was a girl's name or making some remark about my French-Canadian heritage. My friends in Fort Rupert took to calling me "Mishi," after a pet cougar featured in our grade five reader.

In 1966, when MacMillan Bloedel put in a big subdivision on the hillside opposite Robert Scott School, David's stepfather, who was an employee of the company, bought one of the houses.

It was convenient for the children living in those houses to go to school, particularly for David, since he didn't have to get up early and catch the bus from Fort Rupert anymore. There were hardly any Indigenous kids who finished high school, but David did. We graduated in 1971. David was very intelligent and did well in school even though he struggled with his handwriting because he was left-handed, and in elementary school we were forced to learn one particular way to write in cursive script, with the letters leaning to the right. He had to turn his left hand around almost

We didn't feel fully equipped heading into the woods without guns and knives. *Author's collection*

upside down to get the correct angle, but he followed Mrs. Eckley's instructions and did it, even though his handwriting was always kind of difficult to read.

David and I went camping together once. We had heard there was an A-frame cabin on the shore of Georgie Lake, so we decided to head there one nice May weekend. That would have been a few weeks before my thirteenth birthday in June.

We packed up everything we thought we would need for a two-night stay, except a tarp or tent for a shelter, and started walking from our houses to the start of the Holberg road. Of course, we were armed. David had a Mossberg semi-automatic .22 rifle that I greatly admired, and I had my .177-calibre air rifle. How I was going to protect us from cougars and bears with that, I had no idea, but I thought I might be able to pot a grouse.

We started walking up the logging road to Holberg, toward the Georgie Lake turnoff seven miles up, hoping for a ride with some-one heading in that direction, but few vehicles came and those that did roared right by in a cloud of dust. So we had to walk the whole stretch, first to the turnoff and then the next two miles down to the lake. At the lake, a trail followed the shore toward the A-frame.

The trail was not well-used, but it was obvious even though parts of it were boggy. It took about an hour until we finally got to the A-frame. And that is all it was, an A-frame building with cedar shakes for roofing and a very uneven dirt floor.

Neither of us had thought to bring a ground sheet or even a piece of plastic, and all we had for sleeping bags were those thick, heavy padded bags that were available in the 1960s. We found out that night they weren't very warm either.

We gathered up what dryish wood we could from along the shore of the lake and in the woods behind the A-frame and made a fire right inside it, in the fire ring already there on the dirt floor. Of course, the smoke circled around inside the A-frame despite both ends being wide open, and no matter where we sat around the fire we got thoroughly smoked. We heated up whatever it was we brought for food (I'm at a complete blank about what that might have been), and when it got dark, we stretched out on the ground and tried to sleep.

It didn't take much shivering before we realized it was too cold to sleep in those pathetic sleeping bags. We got back up again, and realizing that the rocks in the fire ring were still warm from the fire, we rolled a couple right into the glowing embers remaining of our campfire. When they were good and hot, we rolled them out of the flames with sticks and then tried to get them into our sleeping bags. The smart thing would have been to roll them in a sweater or coat, but we already had everything on that we had brought, so unless we wanted to take something off, we had to sleep with our bare hot rocks. They were hard too, but somehow, we managed to curl up in our bags around our rocks and get some sleep.

The next day, we didn't hang around and hiked back to the road. We were lucky, as someone had come by to pick up a friend of theirs who had arrived in a private float plane, so we got a ride back to Port Hardy in the back of their pickup truck.

Of course, like all the bright, intelligent kids graduating from high school in Port Hardy, we did the smartest thing we could think of to advance our lives and start building a career. We went to work in the woods. Or at least in the forest industry. David did in fact go to work in the woods, starting as a chokerman, but rapidly becoming a rigging slinger and working his way up the hierarchy of the rigging crew. Following my father's advice—"They'll kill you in the rigging"—I joined him on the log boom.

My aim was to save my money and go travelling. David's was to have money to buy things like cars and boats. My girlfriend Pam was also saving to go travelling and she left in September for Europe. Having started working with my dad in June, right out of high school, by Christmas I had enough money to leave for Europe and go travelling too.

David had big dreams when we were teenagers; he wanted to become a fighter pilot in the Israeli air force because he felt that Israel had to be defended. On a more practical level, he also at one time seemed quite serious about joining the RCMP. For a while he was even hanging out at the RCMP detachment and becoming friends with the cops. But at the end of high school, we got jobs.

A few of our friends went off to the University of Victoria for a few months or even a year, but they came back talking about panty raids, getting laid a lot and getting shitfaced drunk. If that was the university experience, I thought, I'd stick to my plan of saving money to go travelling. And I did.

I went to Spain and Africa with Pam in 1972, came back and worked some more, went to Mexico, came back, worked and saved money, split with Pam in 1973 and took off again. I travelled across the Soviet Union on the Trans-Siberian Railway and ended up in Japan. I was living in Sapporo in the early part of 1974 when David asked me to be best man at his wedding. About six months later I was back in Port Hardy, and that's when I met Kimberly.

David was hanging around with a guy named Matt, and they went pit-lamping together, illegally shooting deer at night with spotlights. It was a lot easier than trying to get them in the daylight.

David invited me and this guy to his house for Thanksgiving dinner and Kimberly made her first turkey. And only one, it turns out. She was so nervous and fretting while the bird was in the oven, and us guys were hanging around drinking beer.

The turkey turned out just fine despite Kimberly's nervousness. She was gracious and relieved that everything had turned out okay. She was very young and didn't really have much to say in conversation with three men.

Eventually, the subject turned to guns. David's friend had a small collection and I seemed to recall after dropping in on them one evening when they were skinning some of their pit-lamped deer that he had a Mauser rifle. All I had at the time was my old

.303 Ross rifle and I was in the market for a different gun. So we ended up passing some guns around the living room from hand to hand, and at one point Kimberly asked, "What would happen if you shot yourself with one of those?"

We thought that was just a stupid girl question and Matt answered in kind of a joking manner, "It would take the top of your head off." We thought nothing more of it. We didn't realize it at the time, but she must have been watching closely the way we were working the bolts on the rifles we examined.

I got back to work on the boom with my dad and of course corresponded with my fiancée, Juliane, in Germany, writing to her almost every day and waiting eagerly for her to arrive. It was taking a long time for the Canadian government to approve her immigration status.

Then it happened. It was somewhere in the middle of November when I came home from work and as I came into the house my mother said. "You know what I just heard? David's wife shot herself."

What happened next is still very confusing. I know that David retreated to his parents' house, and that is where he was when I went to see him for the first time after it happened. He was beside himself with grief. He had been to the doctor and been prescribed some antidepressants or whatever, but they didn't seem to do much good.

After the body had been taken away and the house cleaned, I was recruited along with some others, but without David, to go to the house and get some clothes for him and other things. As soon as we walked in, we noticed an overwhelming stench of Pine-Sol. I imagine that there had been an enormous amount of blood in the room where Kimberly had shot herself. It may have been the bedroom. Possibly. I can't remember if the mattress was still on the bed or not, or if there was a hole in the ceiling.

But that smell of Pine-Sol was so strong you knew something horrible must have happened.

It must have been a tremendous shock for David to come home from work, walk into the house, and not being greeted, to look for Kimberly—to walk into the silent house, into the kitchen, into the living room and then the bedroom or wherever she had done it, to find her.

We didn't hang around the house. We looked in the bedroom closet and it was packed with neatly wrapped and labelled Christmas presents for all of David's family. And this was just the beginning of December. We collected them, got what we had to get and got out of there.

Then there was the funeral. Kimberly's mom came for the funeral. She was not very old herself, maybe in her late thirties or early forties. She looked aged with grief, though. Somebody had taken charge and was organizing everything. I think it was somebody named Henderson, a grandson of Vivian Hunt's. Six of David's friends got designated to be pallbearers and we all trooped off to IV's Men's Wear to rent black suits. This was going to be a big funeral.

I remember Henderson went to the airport with a pickup truck and some other guys to pick up the body when it came back from the undertaker. He said he opened the coffin to make sure it was the right body, and it was. He said they had wrapped a kind of turban around her head.

There was a lengthy church service in the Anglican church in Port Hardy. I remember they played "Amazing Grace."

Then there was a convoy of vehicles out to the cemetery at Fort Rupert. We had to extract the coffin from the pickup truck it had been transported in and carefully carry it to the prepared gravesite, where there were several planks laid across the opening of the grave and we gingerly lowered the coffin onto those. It was the first and only time I've ever done that.

There was a huge number of wreaths displayed around the grave as well, including a huge heart made of flowers with "Honey" in more flowers across the middle. No one knew who had sent it.

The minister conducted a lengthy graveside service, and just before we were to lower the coffin into the grave, Kimberly's mother burst from the group of people standing between the minister and the grave and threw herself weeping onto the coffin. Somebody finally extracted her off the coffin, we took our positions with ropes and first lifted the coffin, someone pulled the planks out, and we lowered Kimberly to her final resting place.

At the social gathering after the funeral, Henderson said he was terrified that the coffin and Kimberly's mom were both going to plunge into the grave when she threw herself on it. Fortunately, the planks had held.

My friend David is now buried in that same cemetery.

***

Shortly after Kimberly's funeral my fiancée, Juliane, arrived from Germany, just before Christmas.

We got married on December 28, 1974, almost one year after I had moved in with her in Sapporo, Japan, and we spent much of the next year honeymooning around. We hitchhiked to Vancouver and Victoria, attended a music festival in Duncan, and hung around with friends in Sointula and Alert Bay. We started looking for land on Malcolm Island, where the village of Sointula was located. We even hiked to Cape Scott twice.

At the beginning of 1976 we got to move into a cabin hidden in the woods just on the edge of the flats at the estuary of the Quatse River. It was down a short trail from the old M&B mainline. We had no neighbours, but when summer and salmonberry season arrived, we discovered we had black bears around.

21 / **Bears**

"**Why don't you go** and shoot me a bear?" Juliane said one day. "You keep going out after deer and coming back frustrated and pissed off because you can't get a deer, and there are bears all over the place around here. Why don't you go shoot one of those?"

The week before, we had been invited over to our friends Tom and Andrea's for dinner and they served a nice big bear roast and Juliane loved it. Tom had not deliberately set out to shoot a bear, but one had come sniffing around the floathouse where he lived with his wife and toddler son, Michael. They had a dog too and Tom figured there was just too much chance of conflict or possibly even danger, so he shot the bear. And Juliane loved it when she ate it.

People in Port Hardy in those days didn't shoot bears to eat. The only time most people saw a bear was at the garbage dump, so they just kind of placed bears in the same category as the rats and crows and seagulls feeding on the garbage. Who would possibly want to eat a bear that had been feeding on garbage? I knew very few people who had ever shot a bear.

One was Gary Ewart, our neighbour when I was a kid, and

another I knew of was one Pam's relatives who came up from Washington State to shoot one for the hide. It was probably illegal as hell for a foreigner to come up on an unguided hunt and do that, but nobody knew about it, and if they did, they probably didn't care anyway.

I was at Pam's grandparents' place, where she lived, and there was an odd smell in the house. We asked what that was, and they indicated a big old enamel canner on the stove. "Oh, that's bear meat from when Alex shot that bear," they said. "We're cooking it for the dog."

They hadn't taken care of the meat the way you would if you were slaughtering an animal for the table and had left all the fat on the outside, so the whole house smelled pretty rank.

I had been quite surprised by that bear roast at Tom and Andrea's—it was so tasty.

So I agreed to go and find Juliane a bear.

We lived in a tiny cabin on the outskirts of Port Hardy at the time.

I was working on the log boom in Port McNeill during the week, so one Saturday morning I grabbed my new .243-calibre Remington Model 700 bolt-action rifle and set out looking for a bear for Juliane. She had encouraged me to buy the rifle the year before, when I told her that my first rifle was a World War I relic that had a reputation for blowing back in soldiers' faces.

I walked along the old M&B mainline that went by the trail to our cabin and headed toward the point where it crossed the road to the airport.

There was a chance of seeing a bear right there on the road because salmon were running in the river and bears crossed the road all the time, coming from the bush down to the river. The old mainline was still in very good shape, with tall, old alders on both sides of the road. The leaves carpeted the road and gave off a leathery, tangy smell that only people who have smelled it can recognize.

I crossed the airport road, proceeded only a few hundred yards, then took the overgrown old road that was once called Branch One of the original logging roads.

When I was a kid, logging had already been done on that road and it was the site of the town's garbage dump. You could always see bears there. The dump was long closed down and there wasn't even any evidence of it anymore, except the odd old rusty remnant of an abandoned car left here in the 1950s. The road was barely a track through the tall second-growth trees now.

I had tried to find a bear in there once before. I had been quietly stalking along the road when I hear a loud *"Humph!"* from close and saw a big mother bear only forty yards away from me, shooing a very small cub up a tree and then standing there on two legs looking at me. I had gracefully backed away out of sight and went looking along the river on that occasion.

This time I was very slowly, quietly stalking along the road, which was quite easy because of the thick layer of moss that had grown over the gravel.

I moved ahead one slow step after the other, careful not to make a noise with my feet. I had walked by numerous piles of bear shit, each pile rich with salal berries.

That's when I saw it. I caught a slight movement in the shadows of the trees to my left only about forty yards away, and then it appeared from out of the trees at the edge of the road: a great big black pumpkin-sized head. All I could see was that head, a neck and the front portion of the shoulders. I think the bear looked directly at me, with surprisingly small eyes. My heart jumped in my chest, but then things went very calm as I raised my rifle.

I didn't have a scope on the gun in those days and it was just as well, because at that distance an out-of-focus ball of fur is all I would have seen anyway. I aimed for the middle of the neck and pulled the trigger. My .243 cracked, and the bear disappeared. I lowered the gun and looked, but no bear. I reloaded and

walked slowly toward the spot where the bear had been, and as I,
approached the edge of the road, there it was, lying still under the
tree it had been peeking around. I gingerly poked it in the neck
with the muzzle of my rifle, but there was no response. The beady
little brown eyes were still glassy and bright but lifeless.

I looked down at the big black carcass of the bear, its hide gleam-
ing even in the gloom of the canopy of trees and realized three things.

1. I had never gutted a bear before;
2. It was too big for me to move by myself; and
3. I didn't own a vehicle.

I turned around and walked back to the cabin, told Juliane
that I had shot a bear, dropped my rifle off and then walked/ran
the two or more miles around the bay to Tom and Andrea's. Fortunately, Tom was home, so he piled his kid and dog and a couple
knives into the truck, and we drove over to the mainline, across
the airport road and up Branch One to my bear.

We left the toddler in the cab, but of course the dog jumped
out of the back and immediately ran to the bear, his back all bristly,
and he started barking madly until Tom told him to shut up. Grabbing a front paw each, we pulled the bear up onto the road, the dead
weight of the animal almost more than two of us could handle. But
being young, tough loggers, we pulled it up behind the truck. We
arranged it on its back, and before he started cutting Tom looked
at me and said, "Where's your gun?"

"Oh, back at the cabin." I replied.

He gave me a dirty look but didn't say anything, and so we
rolled the bear onto its back and he started cutting.

When we were done dressing it out, it took all our strength to
lift that bear into the bed of his pickup truck. There was no way we
could just pick it up and toss it in. We lifted the front end up and put
the head and front legs onto the open tailgate, and then, holding it
there as best we could, we got another grip on the fur and hoisted
the back end up, shoving the whole carcass forward.

After driving back to the cabin trail, he and I dragged the bear to the door of the conical addition to the old cabin and then figured out how to hang it on the inside from the rafters. After installing a gambrel between the hind legs, we again needed all our strength to hoist the bear up. Then Tom's volunteer work was done, and the rest was up to Juliane and me.

This must have been around November 4 or 5, because Juliane was nearly nine months pregnant at the time. It was quite a chore getting the hide off the animal, for one thing because it was so long that I had to stand on something to get the cutting started around the back paws and then up the inside of the back legs. Once it was started, the hide peeled off easily enough, though there was so much fat on the back of the bear that we sometimes had a hard time finding where the hide was.

Once it was skinned and hanging, there was the tricky issue of what to do with the meat. My parents forbade us from putting any bear meat in their fridge. Like I said, the attitude in Port Hardy was that bears were just big black rats that ate at the dump, and they didn't want any big black rat meat in their freezer. So Juliane had to can the meat.

I had to go to work five days a week, getting up before daybreak and walking over to the road to catch the crummy to Port McNeill, where I worked on the log boom. But as soon as my parents had told us we couldn't put the bear meat in the freezer, we started gathering canning jars and lids. I don't know if my mom was generous enough to provide the jars or if we had to buy them all new or what, but we eventually got plenty of jars and lids and started cutting up the bear. And that is what Juliane did while I was away at work. She had the oil stove going full bore, first roasting pans full of bear meat in the oven, then cooling it and putting it in jars that she canned in a big enamel canner on top of the stove while the next batch of meat was being roasted. In her limited spare time, she managed to render down all the fat from the bear and put it in gallon jars from the beer parlour. They sold pickled eggs and sausages there to drunks who didn't bother going home for dinner. We ended up with nine gallons of clear rendered bear grease that we used as boot grease on my caulk boots and diaper rash ointment, and for cooking and deep-frying doughnuts.

I would come home to an exhausted, nine-months-pregnant Juliane in a steamy cabin full of the scent of fresh-roasted bear meat.

Juliane kept this up day after day until she was literally ready to pop. When she got down to the last hind quarter of bear meat, she just couldn't do it anymore, so she packed up the hindquarter into her backpack that she had brought from Germany barely two years earlier and went to the road to hitchhike to Port Hardy to try and sneak the meat into my parents' freezer after all.

After our daughter Jessica was born on November 10, 1976, I took some time off in the summer of 1977 to go to Europe and introduce her to Juliane's family and friends. When we got back, we wanted to eat some of the last piece of frozen bear meat, because everything else was canned. When we looked in the freezer, it was gone. We asked my parents what happened to that hindquarter of bear meat we'd left in the freezer.

"Oh, there was no bear meat in the freezer," my mom said. "There was a big moose roast that Nick gave us and we cooked it. It was really good."

So that was the end of our only opportunity to eat any of the bear from the freezer, and we went back to our plentiful canned supply in our little cabin on the flats.

22 / Flats Cabin

IN EARLY 1976 WE MOVED INTO Buster Benjamin's old cabin, tucked into the bush just off the M&B mainline on the flats. Buster was gone by then and the cabin had been occupied by Robert and Mavis, a couple who had moved to Port Hardy while I was abroad and meeting Juliane in Japan.

I had come back from travelling in September 1974 and set up the immigration process with the immigration office in Nanaimo, and Juliane had come at Christmas. We spent nearly all of 1975 living at my parents' house, but that became intolerable, and we ended up house-sitting at friends' places while they were away.

It was while we were staying at my ex-girlfriend Pam's house over the 1975 Christmas and New Year holiday, when Pam was away in California, that Robert and Mavis stopped by the floathouse in their restored 1951 International Harvester pickup truck. I still remember how elegant Mavis looked in her big tweed overcoat. They were both examples of perfect hippie sartorial elegance.

"Do you want our house?' Robert said bluntly through his beard. "We're going to India."

Holy smoke! That sounded ideal. Robert and Mavis had more than doubled the size of Buster's plain little shingled, one-room cabin with a mushroom-shaped, cedar-shake-covered addition that provided a lot of storage space for supplies, clothing and boots, with room to spare. As soon as they cleared out of there, we checked with the property owner, David O'Connor, agreed to pay the annual rent of a bottle of Irish whisky a year, and moved in.

To enter the cabin you walked up a couple of steps and through a big handmade wooden door and into the addition, which was built to the right of the old, shingled cabin. Inside, the addition opened to the right, and if you turned left, there was the entrance to the original cabin.

Opening the door to the cabin, you realized how small it was. Immediately to the right was a large oil stove, then a small sink and counter. To the left of the door was a small shelving unit, and at the opposite end of the cabin, which was barely sixteen feet long, a small bunk on either side of the room.

It was obvious that it would have been comfortable for a single old bachelor, but even for a couple it was cramped. Only one person could stand up and move around and do things in the cabin at a time.

Robert had lined the inside walls with cedar shakes, the same as those on the outside of the addition. One of these shakes had a stash hole for drugs. Hash and marijuana were illegal and could earn you serious jail time if caught in possession.

That oil stove was hot. Even turned all the way down, the heat was almost unbearable inside. We often wore very little clothing and sometimes none, it was so hot, which freaked some people out if they came to the door for a visit. Seeing as the tank for the stove was situated right at the road so the fuel delivery guy could fill it up, we started having a problem with people stealing the oil. They were using it in their trucks, I suppose, because fuel oil for stoves and diesel fuel are so similar. This happened several times before I went to the local machinist who just happened to be our first neighbour on the flats, in the old Holmgren house, and got some U-shaped bolts welded onto the fuel caps and then secured these with an iron bar and a padlock, to keep from being ripped off. All I had to do was provide the fuel man with a key. Solved that problem.

Facilities were basic at the cabin. We had to haul water from the nearby creek and keep some in the house to use. We always had a big ten-gallon galvanized container on the stove to have hot water on hand. Toilet facilities were also very basic, with an outhouse out the back in Buster's old garden.

The soil was very fertile there, seeing as it was the ancient estuary of the Quatse River, which entered the ocean half a mile away. Buster had always had an excellent garden, and my father had also got permission from him to garden there when he was still alive, clearing away the salmonberries on the other side of the creek for a substantial garden. Robert and Mavis had a garden there, and when spring 1976 came along, we prepared the soil and made our very first garden together there too.

There was good garden soil right in front of the cabin, where we grew peas. We had quite a few problems with Steller's jays coming and pulling up the peas, so I shot one with my air rifle and hung it from a tall pole over the peas as a warning to the others. But it wasn't long before the carcass disappeared off the pole, so I shot another one and did the same thing. And the same thing happened.

The ground was soft in the garden and the tracks in the soil identified the culprit: a black bear. There were always bears around that part of the outskirts of Port Hardy, even more so in the fall when the salmon were running. But this was the summer, and they were more scattered in the hills all around, eating berries.

One time, Juliane said she was walking along the road toward our place, on her way back from shopping, and there were two small bears feeding by the side of the road, a yearling and a very small cub. Their mothers must have been shot, and having found each other, they had bonded like siblings. The road had once been a very wide, well-maintained logging road, the M&B mainline, but it was no longer used, so in addition to being hugely potholed, it was lined with the bushes that had gotten thicker and thicker. In late spring and early summer, the salmonberries ripened and were a delicious treat for the bears. So they didn't notice her until she was almost right up to them. Then the larger one caught a sniff of her scent, woofed loudly and cuffed the little one in the butt to get him moving, and they both dived straight through the salmonberries into the alders beyond.

***

Juliane got pregnant while we were in the cabin. We know exactly what day she got pregnant too, because our friends Yuri and Maureen were staying with us, sleeping in the single bunk on the other side of the one-room cabin from us, and we didn't want to have sex while we had guests literally an arm's-length away from us.

But it was February 14, Valentine's Day, and as a special gift for me Juliane bought a fretless electric bass guitar off Yuri. He had given up on bass playing and was concentrating on learning the banjo. So that night the inevitable happened, and for the next nine months we gestated a baby while living in the cabin.

I was working on the log boom for M&B in Port McNeill at the time, having got the job in December at the end of 1975, after our year of honeymooning.

Juliane didn't like Port Hardy very much, so we started looking for property to buy on Malcolm Island, home of the settlement of Sointula.

We spent the spring of 1976, when I had time off, working on the garden, turning over the sod in places that hadn't been worked on in a while and planting, planning for our harvest in the fall. Of course, we were expecting the most important harvest of our lives in November. We didn't have a clue what to expect as expectant parents, but of course who does? It is as if humans must learn how to rear children all over again, with every generation. The only guide we have is how our parents raised us.

Meanwhile, also in our spare time, we continued going to Sointula when we could and negotiated to buy ten acres of land off some older American friends of mine who had come to Sointula in the 1960s. They were interested in subdividing forty acres of their eighty-acre parcel into four ten-acre lots, so we agreed to buy one of them once the subdivision was approved.

I continued working on the boom in Port McNeill five days a week throughout the year. I was skinny, barely 125 pounds, and was eating enormous amounts of food to fuel myself up for the work down on the boom. Some guys got to run boats, and I did too, driving the sidewinder to shove bundles of logs around, but that was mostly for the older guys, so I was one of the main labourers who had to be shoving things around with a pike pole, pulling swifter wires across the boom or fighting with heavy steel boom chains to make up sets of boomsticks. Juliane still recalls that she would make a massive amount of spaghetti for dinner, for example; we would each eat a portion and then I would eat the remaining, usually extra-large portion for breakfast before heading off to work.

One Saturday, when Juliane was nine months pregnant and finished processing the big bear I shot, I was home and Juliane was writing a letter to her mother back in Germany. I stepped out to have a leak and there was a spike buck right there in the garden, not twenty feet away from me. I stepped back into the cabin and grabbed my rifle and a couple of cartridges and gingerly stepped outside. The deer was still there, but nervous now at all my activity. He slowly started walking up the left-hand path to the road. We had a second path to the road on the right, so I took that one. About halfway to the road, only about fifty yards along, the paths almost met, and I saw the deer through the salmonberry bushes, and he saw me, so he doubled back toward the house. So did I, and we met back at the garden, where we had first seen each other. He stood completely still, barely twenty feet away from me, so I raised the rifle, sighted for the middle of his neck, and fired. He dropped.

Juliane burst out of the cabin door, her eyes wide with alarm, almost popping out of her head. "What was... that?" she said, her voice shaking, and then she saw the buck lying out in the garden. "Oh. I see."

She had been comfortably writing the letter home and hadn't even noticed me grab my gun. She was just writing that she was so thankful to be finished all the hard work of processing the bear and now could hopefully look forward to a few days' rest before having the baby. Then *bang*, and she just about jumped out of her skin.

She was also upset at me for making more work, but the deer was tiny compared with the bear. And besides, my parents weren't prejudiced against deer meat in their freezer, so we were able to cut it and freeze it at their place.

***

Fish were both a boon and a bane at the cabin.

I had known since childhood that there was a run of creek sockeye going up the Quatse River, just across the road from the trail to our cabin. The salmon swam up the Quatse River and spawned in the tributaries above the lake. They were small for sockeye salmon—a large one would have been around four pounds—but they were deep-red-fleshed and very tasty. It was a popular activity to go down to a likely-looking pool and jig these fish out when they were migrating upstream, because they were unlikely to bite any lure. Jigging, which involved attaching one or more large treble hooks to the end of a usually weighted line, meant casting the hooked arrangement into the pool and dragging it across the bottom or midwater and jerking on it periodically in order to snag the fish. It was highly illegal, of course, and the fisheries officer was always on the lookout for this. But the fish ran upstream at the same time as the Stanley Cup playoffs, so when there was a playoff game on, serious jiggers would go down to the river and jig sockeye.

Sometimes people would go there first thing in the morning before work and try their luck. One time, on my way home from work, there were no cars parked opposite my trail, so I walked down to the river's edge to see if there was any sign of activity that had taken place that day. After a quick look for tracks on the river-bank, I happened to look at a gap under a washed-up, bleached tree on the bank and there was a still very fresh sockeye lying there. So I took it home for dinner.

In the fall of even-numbered years, the pink salmon came back in huge numbers. This was 1976, so by early October they were flooding into the river. They were there by the thousands, so I didn't feel bad about jigging one or two of those out of the river. The flesh of returning pink salmon isn't very good, but if you catch a silvery-skinned one, the flesh can be edible.

I came home from work one day, and Juliane, eight and a half months pregnant, was half-smoking, half-baking three salmon she'd caught, over the firepit near the house. Even the little creek right beside the cabin was full of fish, which swam by and spawned a little farther up.

After our daughter was born on November 10, though, and Juliane came back home with the newborn Jessica, the fish in the creek became a problem. After spawning, they died in the creek and lay there by the thousands, rotting. That was our fresh-water supply for drinking and cooking, and now, with a new baby, we needed clean water to rinse and wash the diapers in too.

I got a garden fork and started patrolling the creek, pitching the carcasses out onto the banks for as far as I could walk in the tunnel of salmonberry that arched over the water. Sometimes I had to bend over double just to get through. It was just a tiny little creek, but boy did it harbour thousands of fish.

The dead fish were great for the garden, that was for sure. I think Buster and my father after him had buried lots of carcasses in that garden across the creek, and this, with the rich alluvial soil already there, made it grow excellent vegetables.

We sometimes thought that old Buster's ghost came back to haunt us.

I can't remember if it was me or Yuri, when he and Maureen were staying with us—but in any event, one of us was changing strings on a guitar, and one of the keeper plugs that secure the strings in place in the bridge popped out and disappeared. We just could not find it for love or money. We checked both beds, under the pillows, the floor, shelves, countertops, stove top, everywhere. That little plug was gone, gone, gone, so we carved one out of wood and used that to secure the string in place.

And then one day, six months later, that little string retainer appeared in the middle of our kitchen counter. Where did that come from? Did Buster find it and return it to us? We'll never know.

***

Port Hardy had by now gotten bigger and rowdier than I was comfortable with. It wasn't the quiet, isolated little logging town I had grown up in. It had outgrown me or I had outgrown it. The Island Highway to the south was open now, but had not been completely paved yet; the mine was booming, the cannery was going full bore during salmon and herring seasons, various logging companies had filled in the gap M&B left behind, and it was just getting too crowded. Besides that, we were eager to own something rural of our own where we could build a house and have a garden, and property like that was not available in Port Hardy. It was all organized, instant subdivisions, which we found distasteful.

We purchased ten acres of land on Malcolm Island from my friends Larry and Carol and planned to move to Sointula as soon as we could to start clearing an acre of the forested property.

We stayed in that little cabin until our daughter Jessica was almost one year old in 1977, and then moved to a rented house in Sointula and started cutting trees down on our land to make room for the new home we planned to build.

Acknowledgements

I AM GRATEFUL FOR all the assistance provided by the following people, in person or in published interviews: Craig Aspinall, Paula Brink, Catherine C. Carlson, Margo Chapman, Kempton Dexter, Mickey Flanagan, Alan Haig-Brown, Rick James, Rolf Leben, John Nicholson, Daryl, Lillian, Melanie and Joyce O'Connor, Cliff Manson, Rick Marcotte, Bruce Melan, Les Melan, Jim Lyon, John Lyon, Tom Masterman, Brenda McCorquodale, Sally McMahon, Diane Toth, James Walkus and Ollie Walkus. Any errors in historical facts or details are all mine alone.

I have mostly used people's real names throughout this book. In a few cases demanding discretion, I have altered the names of some individuals.

I am also indebted to the books *A Dream Come True*, published by the Port Hardy Heritage Society, *Yesterday's Promises*, by David Lewis, *The Story of Island Copper*, by Craig Aspinall, and *Port Hardy and District*, edited by Harold and Irene Pym, as well as to the *North Island Gazette* archives and the blog *The Undiscovered Coast*, by Brenda McCorquodale.

This book would not have been possible without the encouragement and support offered at Harbour Publishing by Howard White, Anna Comfort O'Keeffe, Caroline Skelton, Colleen Bidner and the very patient and thorough editor Brian Lynch.

And, of course, I am deeply thankful to my wife and partner of fifty years, Juliane, for her unwavering support and putting up with me vanishing into my tiny upstairs office and neglecting the vegetable garden for four years, letting the weeds take over while I finished this book.